Date: 9/24/15

658.409 SIM
Simpson, Jo
The restless executive :
reclaim your values, love

'I love this book. Because it is written as a story, I was totally captivated all the way through, and had a lot of valuable insights along the way. It helped me confront some of my own restlessness and take a deeper look at what my most important values are and make a new commitment to live them more fully. I highly recommend it to anyone who isn't totally satisfied with your work or your life.'

Jack Canfield, Bestselling Author and Co-Creator of Chicken Soup for the Soul™

'The Restless Executive provides much needed guidance on how to lead organizations in the new democratic age at work. Jo offers a blueprint on how to lead with purpose and from the heart. This is much needed for all leaders today.'

Miranda Ash, Chief Community Evangelist, WorldBlu

'Too many professionals suffer a huge disconnect between what they do every day and what they truly want out of life. Read Jo Simpson's *The Restless Executive* to link your daily life to your values – you'll find yourself re-energized and content at the same time!'

Marshall Goldsmith, International Bestselling Author of *What Got You Here Won't Get You There, Thinkers 50* Top Ten Global Business Thinker and top ranked executive coach

'Jo is an incredible coach whom I would (and indeed have done so) recommend without hesitation to anyone that would benefit from a personal transformation. She's clearly passionate about helping others achieve their full potential. *The Restless Executive* serves as a highly valuable extension of her incredible work.'

Paul Callaghan, FCA, Partner, Audit, KPMG

'This fast-moving book puts you in touch with the most important qualities of leaders: they know who they are, what they believe, and they don't compromise.'

Brian Tracy, Bestselling Author of *Eat That Frog!* and *How the Best Leaders Lead*

'*The Restless Executive* is an important book for leaders questioning their path. The practical tools and tips support you to work in a way that's more in line with your values. This creates the powerful and positive intervention which is the missing piece many leaders are seeking.'

Helen Tupper, Head of Consumer, Virgin Management

'It's true that you will read this book and recognize yourself in the story if you have ever questioned the way you operate. Jo captures the essence of what it really means to live and lead from your core values and how that will truly transform the impact of your leadership, whilst enriching the experience of those around you.'
Jeremy Bevan, Vice President, EMEAR Marketing, Cisco

'Whether you are a 'restless executive' or not, Jo Simpson's inspiring book explains how your core values can guide you to a more fulfilling life, both at work, and at home. Read it and work towards what you want to be.'
Michael Woodhead, Chief Executive, HCP

'I loved this book! Jo tells a wonderful universal story with incisiveness, wisdom and humour. She articulates beautifully the heroic journey we are all on to show up with our authentic Self and our true values in the world. Read this book and be inspired, validated and guided to unwrapping more of who you truly are so you will be happier and the world will benefit from who you truly are.'
Nick Williams, Bestselling Author of nine books, including *The Work We Were Born to Do*

'In *The Restless Executive* Jo Simpson takes a complex subject and explains it in a way that is so easily relatable that I am sure there are plenty of 'restless executives' who will recognize themselves in this interesting journey of a book. This insightful book allows you to intimately follow William Cleverley's journey of transformation and perhaps think about how you too can engage in a process of self-discovery. Using *The Restless Executive*, Jo Simpson shows us that there really is a different way to work and live.'
Karen Fisher, Head of HR, HCP

'What a great book! Jo Simpson has really pulled it off here – a page turning and well written story that entertains and educates in equal measure. Within a few pages I found myself very quickly drawn into William Cleverley's journey and perhaps uncomfortably at times, recognized elements of my own on-going leadership challenge. I felt compelled to keep the pages turning but and ultimately *The Restless Executive* is a hugely thought provoking and uplifting book. This is a rare thing for me – a business read that will stay in my mind for a long time; a story that resonates at many levels with many powerful ideas and tips to come back to again and again. If I take one thing away, it's that changing the way you lead really is possible when you act positively on the core values that define who you are. I am sure that leaders the world over will take their own meaning and benefit from Jo's work.'
Paul Meneely, HR Director, Cavendish Nuclear

'There are plenty of restless executives who will recognize themselves in this brilliant book. Through eloquent storytelling, Jo Simpson demonstrates that by reclaiming your values you really can be true to yourself, lead with purpose and love what you do.'
Keith Robson, Senior Director, Learning and Organisation Development (L&OD), eBay Global Marketplaces

'This brilliant parable will help you discover who you truly are at your core and support you to lead with courage. *The Restless Executive* is perfect for people who are feeling overwhelmed, frustrated and struggling with the constant day-to-day demands placed on them.'
Dave Sharpe, Event Host, BBC Broadcaster and Communications Specialist

'*The Restless Executive* is the road map to becoming who you truly want to be and accomplishing your ultimate goals! Within these pages you will learn how to re-align yourself with your core values and shift your perspective to get in touch with who you really are and become who you really want to be. If your aim is to evolve and grow as an individual so you'll be empowered to lead with courage and reach new heights of success, fulfillment, and purpose, you need to read this book.'
Ivan Misner, Ph.D., *NY Times* Bestselling Author and Founder of BNI®

'If you choose only one book to support you in your personal journey to find and be the authentic 'you', you should make it this one. Through the story of William, Jo Simpson poses thought provoking questions for today's executives - many of whom will empathize with William's corporate world. By exploring how we choose to honour and embed our core values in all aspects of life, Jo offers a compelling invitation for personal change and self-fulfilment. A truly uplifting read full of encouragement and practical ideas.'
Jennifer Whitehill, Head of Talent Management E.ON UK HR

For

The Restless Executive in us all...

&

To all of those I have had the pleasure of working with – thank you for being open to the journey of self-discovery, courageous leadership and for being prepared to **'go there'**!

The Restless Executive

Reclaim your values, love what you do and lead with purpose

Jo Simpson

WILEY

Registered office

John Wiley and Sons Ltd, The Atrium, Southern Gate, Chichester, West Sussex, PO19
8SQ, United Kingdom

For details of our global editorial offices, for customer services and for information
about how to apply for permission to reuse the copyright material in this book please see
our website at www.wiley.com.

Library of Congress Cataloging-in-Publication Data

Simpson, Jo (Business consultant)
  The restless executive : reclaim your values, love what you do and lead with purpose /
Jo Simpson.
      pages cm
  ISBN 978-1-119-07121-1 (cloth) ISBN 978-1-119-07122-8 (ePDF)
  ISBN 978-1-119-07123-5 (epub)
1. Executives–Psychology. 2. Management. 3. Executive coaching. I. Title.
  HD38.2.S55 2015
  658.4'09–dc23

                              2015005265

Cover Design: Wiley
Cover Image: ©Kostsov/Shutterstock

Set in 10.5/14 and Adobe Caslon by SPi-Global, Chennai, India
Printed in Great Britain by TJ International Ltd, Padstow, Cornwall

CONTENTS

CONTENTS

Introduction

THIS BOOK IS A MUST READ IF:

You are an executive, a manager or member of a team and you are feeling unhappy, challenged, unsatisfied, bored or restless

You are fed up with the way things are done and know deep down that there is another way, but not sure exactly what that is

You are already doing great work and want to take yourself, team or organization to the next level

A feeling of 'Restlessness' is stirring in today's corporate world. Leaders of all levels are experiencing it and starting to question what they do and why they do it, aside from habitual material drives. Intuitively they already know that there's a different way to operate, to show up and to positively influence others, yet until now there hasn't been a road map to show them how...

Throughout my work as a Keynote Speaker and Executive Leadership Coach, I have seen first hand the transformation that can be achieved when a person truly understands the power of their core values and lives and leads in alignment with them.

The Restless Executive tells the story of William Cleverley, the Operations Director at a well-respected global consultancy firm, Gant Foster, which is currently going through a company rebrand and repositioning. Struggling with the excessive day-to-day demands and pressures of the business, William feels overwhelmed and frustrated. He has reached a crossroads in his life, with the dawning realization that what used to be important to him no longer seems to feel of any real value. He has ignored the 'intuitive nudges' urging him to make changes – at least, up until now.

He is at a point where he knows something has to give, but doesn't know what or how, and he thinks his only option is to leave the company. However, at some level, William is already awakening to a new sense of being. He has developed a certain level of awareness compared to most of his colleagues. He is naturally curious and is more in touch with his gut instinct than he first realizes. This enables him to operate from the heart more fully and not just from the head.

As he begins his journey of transformation from Restless Executive to Courageous Leader, William engages in a process of self-discovery that helps him change his personal and professional life forever.

While the characters and events in *The Restless Executive* are purely fictional and not based on any individual, you may recognize aspects of yourself in William, as he is representative of so many restless leaders in today's modern world.

SUGGESTIONS FOR HOW TO GET THE MOST OUT OF THIS BOOK ...

In addition to following William's journey, this book is also a practical guide to explore your own restlessness and discover the gifts that it holds.

I invite you to read William's story on two levels – both as a story and as a way to learn more about yourself. From Chapter 4 onwards, you will find questions at the end of each chapter, which will help you discover who *you* truly are at your core.

I encourage you to work through the questions in a sequential order initially as they follow William's transformation, from a Restless Executive to a Courageous Leader.

The questions have been designed to build on each other, leading you towards transformation, should you choose to '*go there*'.

I also highly recommend that you invest in a journal or notebook to take notes, as you embark on this journey of self discovery and reflection.

You may also choose to dip in and out of the book on a regular basis, exploring its many practical tips, tools and techniques that can help you transform the way you live, lead, and show up in the world.

Let the journey begin.....

PART I

The Disconnect

'There is a gift in your restlessness – discover it, for it holds the key to transformation.'

I

A Moment of Realization

It was the evening of the annual 'Leaders of Tomorrow' awards dinner. A glittering black-tie affair held at The Dorchester hotel, London, attended by over 2000 employees gathered from Gant Foster's European offices. There were representatives from all levels of the business, including board members and non-executive directors, many of whom William Cleverley, the company's Operations Director, looked up to and whose admiration he sought.

William had been asked to present an award. It was his big chance, an opportunity to shine but the importance of the event was making him unusually nervous, as he adjusted his bow-tie for the umpteenth time. This was one of the most prestigious events in the Gant Foster annual calendar and until now William had simply been too busy to give it due attention. It was only yesterday that he'd so much as thought about what to say and had haphazardly drawn up his speech. He was now just moments away from being called to the stage.

William fidgeted in his seat, as Melissa Jacobs, the European Marketing Director, presented the award for the most Innovative

Advertising Idea. His category for the Rising Star Award was up next. He sighed a long breath of desperation.

Watching Melissa, he marvelled at how clearly she spoke, concisely explaining the history of the award and acknowledging all the entrants for their brilliant ideas. 'Well it's been an incredibly close call, but I am delighted to announce that tonight's winner is Susan Dillon, for her highly visual and engaging campaign, as celebrated in so many industry publications already this year.'

William's face turned ashen white as Melissa eloquently described why Susan was such a worthy winner, placing great emphasis on her achievements and why she was so proud of Susan and her team. What's more, she had already brilliantly summarised the strengths of each shortlisted entrant. Not a single member of the audience could be in any doubt that Melissa cared about her nominees ... she'd focused her speech entirely on them.

William, on the other hand, was about to do the opposite. Caught up in his own self-importance, he'd planned to share his personal success story to show the winner what they might expect as a result of their triumph. What on earth had he been thinking? How could he so foolishly have overlooked that the event was about recognizing the award nominees for their successes and achievements rather than his own rise to glory through the company? It was thinly veiled self-promotion at best, and he feared this could really backfire on him. He'd been so wrapped up with concerns about his own public image and how to use this precious opportunity to make an impression, that he'd quite forgotten himself and was behaving like a total idiot. Why did he think his story mattered anyway? Did he really crave recognition that desperately?

Beads of sweat formed on his temple and he wished he'd done more preparation, but it was too late for that now. He tried to reassure himself that as this wasn't the first speech he'd given, everything would surely be okay? Of course it would … he'd be fine and the words would flow naturally. His anxiety had grown a little during the extravagant dinner – the long wait until his scheduled slot had given him far too much time to dwell, and now, having heard Melissa, he was taking deep breaths to calm the tension building inside him. All he wanted was to get out there and get the whole thing over with.

As Eric, a Senior Vice President at Gant Foster and William's seemingly hard-to-please boss, was welcomed back on stage, William realized that the time had come for him to stand in front of 2000 people to present the award. What the hell was he going to do now? He hadn't researched any of the nominees and didn't have a clue what to say. He was resigned to thinking that nothing good could come of this, and that he was about to make a complete fool of himself. He'd well and truly blown it, his career and reputation were surely on the line.

Eric paused, looked up from behind the lectern, and in a clear and authoritative voice made his announcement: 'Ladies and gentlemen, it's now time for the Rising Star Award, and to make the presentation would you please give a warm welcome to our Operations Director, William Cleverley!'

Applause filled the room as William rose from his seat. It was only a short distance to the stage, but he was amazed at the stream of destructive thoughts racing through his mind as he walked up the steps towards Eric. How on earth was he going to pull this off and salvage his dignity? Riding the feeling of anxiety in his chest, he took another deep breath to ease the palpitations. If only he could wake up and discover this was just a bad dream.

William shook Eric's hand and turned to face the expectant audience, but before he had a chance to lean forward towards the microphone, Eric squeezed in front of him and began speaking again. 'Ladies and gentlemen, to me William is a role model employee and I had no hesitation in giving him the honour of presenting this award. As a former winner in this category you can be sure he knows exactly what it takes to succeed at Gant Foster. Please give him another big round of applause!' William cringed. Eric's spontaneous address had put him so high on the company pedestal that he could surely only plummet from here. If he'd only known before why Eric had chosen him for this honour he'd have realized those reasons alone gave him the recognition he desired. He hardly needed to make some lofty speech to big himself up, Eric had more than adequately fluffed his peacock feathers, and ironically – for once he wished he hadn't.

A nervous smile flickered across William's face as he loosened his collar and reached for the gold envelope. The bright spotlights picked out the redness in his cheeks as he self-consciously wiped his clammy palms down the sides of each trouser leg.

'Good evening, it's a wonderful privilege to be here,' spluttered William, unconvincingly. He forced a smile, wishing he were invisible. His mind had frozen. Totally blank, he stared out at the expectant sea of faces as a flash of panic surged in his chest. Deliberately fixing his stare above the audience's heads, he waited for the words to come…but nothing came. He could feel his body starting to tremble. And then he spoke, just blurting out whatever words came and hoping for the best. 'I know how hard you … that is the shortlisted finalists, err … must have worked to, err, get this far.' William's mind seized up again.

'Err, I'm certain there are some outstanding candidates,' he blustered. All the names on the nomination list completely escaped him. He was totally lost for words. The audience fixed their gaze on him and at that precise moment William felt like he was lined up to face a 2000-strong firing squad. Eric could barely watch as William went from bad to worse.

How much more embarrassing could this get, wondered Eric? Why hasn't he rehearsed? Heck, how would it reflect on him now after his big introduction? 'Just open the envelope,' he snapped brusquely.

William nodded, quickly tearing at the thin paper to unveil the card within. 'Please put your hands together for an excellent guy, Jason Goodman,' he announced the winner, failing to hide the tremble in his voice. It was clear he'd blatantly overlooked what Jason had actually done to merit the award.

William stood dumbfounded on the front of the stage, frantically searching for the right words to say next. But his mind had deserted him, crashed. Nowhere to go. 'F****ck!' his whole being cried inside. And he just stood there, grinning inanely at the audience for what felt like an inordinately long time. He felt a rush of dizziness, his eyes glazed over and the whole room became a complete blur.

Eric assumed control and beckoned Jason over to give his acceptance speech. He was eager to make it as seamless as possible and save William any further embarrassment ... he was, after all, a key member of his team. And he could always find out why things had gone so wrong later. William hurried off to the wings where his good friend Steve was waiting, his face wrought with concern.

'What happened William?' he asked, trying not to sound too overtly concerned. 'That's not like you. Is everything okay?'

'Not now thanks Steve,' William retorted, raising his hand. 'I need to be alone.'

Head down, William marched purposefully towards the toilets. He heard his name called out more than once, but he just ignored it and hurried on into the Gents, eager to avoid any interactions.

Standing over the washbasin, he wondered what he could possibly say to explain his behaviour. He threw more cold water over his face, wiped it dry and stood staring at his pitiful reflection in the mirror. He barely recognized the wretch that stared back at him, eyes full of fear and black bags ringing his eyes. 'You complete and utter buffoon,' he cursed, hammering the hand-dryer with his fist and wincing at the pain that flared in his knuckles.

William headed surreptitiously for the bar. Ordering a double whiskey, he raised the glass in his trembling hand and quickly downed the drink in one, signalling for the barman to pour him another. He felt a hand on his shoulder.

'William,' said Steve, as William turned to face him. 'Are you okay buddy? What happened out there?'

William was still trembling. 'I don't know Steve. I just lost it, I guess. I feel terrible for Jason, and furious with myself for letting Eric down like that. Not to mention making a total fool of myself! I've really messed up big time here Steve,' William sighed. 'I'm going home.' He slugged back the second whiskey and slamming the glass down on the bar, he started to walk away.

'Hey hey, not so fast.' Steve placed a reassuring hand on William's shoulder. 'Just wait here a moment, you're in no fit state to go anywhere just yet. Now just breathe. That's it. And again ...'

After a few minutes, William appeared to be a little calmer. 'Steve, I've been such an idiot. I've messed up good and proper this time ... I don't know what happened back there. I feel like I'm losing the plot.'

'It's okay,' Steve assured him. 'You're exhausted and completely stressed out! You've been pushing yourself too hard, for too long – something had to give. Maybe this is a blessing in disguise … an opportunity for you to stop and take stock of what's happening? Unless, of course, you're happy to be heading for burnout or something much worse? Trust me, I recognize the signs well … The choice is yours.'

'I'm not sure I know what you're talking about Steve. And as for choice, I'm not so sure I have got one, besides – Eric's surely going to want to fire me, right?' William sighed trying to relieve the tightness in his chest. 'My career could be in ruins and my life feels totally out of control. I feel like I have gone right over the edge and this is the final straw!'

'You always have a choice, William. It may not feel like it, but you ALWAYS have a choice. It doesn't have to be this way.'

Steve apologized for sounding harsh, but it was for William's own good. Sometimes you have to be cruel to be kind no matter what, especially when someone's health could be at stake.

Steve knew this all too well. He was the Product Development Director at Gant Foster and had been back at work for just three months after suffering a heart attack last year. This had been a huge shock to everyone in the company when it happened, after all Steve was only 44 at the time (three years younger than William was now) and had seemed so in control. Nothing ever appeared to faze him on the surface and he was always the one to pull the team through with a smile on his face, whatever the circumstances.

William sighed again. 'You know what Steve – work and tonight's monumental cock up aside, I've been a terrible husband to Rebecca lately, and no better a father to the kids. I haven't made time for Rebecca, for us, and I think my kids are just paying me lip service these days. And I even missed Tom's concert last week and he had a solo piano part! I just completely forgot about it and then I was out of favour with everyone at home – and quite rightly so. I'm missing out on my children growing up – and for what exactly? Where the hell did I go so wrong? I feel like no one seems to understand me any more, least of all myself. My head has been so far up my own backside that I seem to have totally lost all perspective.'

'Well maybe you're having a wake up call and it's simply time to make some changes. But right now, let's get you home. Come on, I'll drive you.'

'You can't drive, you've had too much to drink'

'I was drinking sparkling water all evening. I've changed a lot of my habits and daily practices. Having a heart attack does that for you ... let's hope you don't get to that stage.'

Feeling a shooting pain in his chest, William wondered if a heart attack wasn't too much of a distant possibility for him, right here and now.

'Keep breathing, William. Take some deep breaths and don't say another word,' said Steve as they pulled away in the car.

William felt numb, but had managed to compose himself a little by the time he returned home to his wife. His chest pains were easing, thankfully, but he remembered an inner feeling he'd simply dismissed … an inner feeling of foreboding, a warning that he was heading for trouble. He couldn't carry on like this … if he didn't stop and make changes, life would do it for him, judging by what Steve was saying, but William could make no sense of anything right now.

'You're fortunate it wasn't a serious health scare that gave you this wake up call,' said Steve, almost reading William's mind. 'And only time will tell if that's what this is. It took a heart attack to make me stop and think. You have already had the warning signs, now you've just been delivered a moment of realization and have a clear choice to make. You can change or you can carry on as before and wait until it's too late. Please do something about it NOW or your health will get worse – you're already exhausted. Who knows what this could lead to and then what use will you be to anyone, especially yourself? Life gives us little signs or "nudges" and if we don't listen to them, it finds a way of making us stop. They don't even have to be major or dramatic events, it can be the smallest thing that makes us wake up. If we don't listen to these nudges, to that voice inside of us that somehow seems to know, we do so at our peril. Listen to your gut or intuition as I now call it, William, please!'

Steve realized he was being a little hard-hitting and was unsure if the timing was right for this conversation, but he wanted to really make William think. They drove the rest of the way in silence, giving William time to reflect. He definitely felt some resistance towards Steve's hippy intuition spiel and yet he couldn't help thinking he might be onto something, somehow it resonated. Perhaps he had been ignoring the signs…perhaps that was where he had gone so wrong.

As William got out of the car, Steve turned to him. 'I know it feels like this is the worst thing in the world right now, but tomorrow you can put this into perspective and see it as a chance to make some positive and obviously overdue changes. And you don't have to do all of this on your own. I am currently working with someone who can perhaps help you too, an executive coach. The work we are doing really is very empowering – there is a different way.' And with that Steve left. He had just wanted to give William some hope amongst all of this upset. He would talk to him again in the next few days when hopefully William had calmed down.

Steve had received his own 'nudges' in the past which he regretted not acting on. He certainly didn't want William to make the same mistake. He was well aware that something, in his case a heart attack, could stop you in your tracks and force you to change. He wished he'd made a choice to change earlier. Still, he was where he was, and he'd learned a lot since then, especially to live in the present with as much gratitude as possible, for all that he had.

At this moment in time he was grateful he could be there for William.

* * *

'It's your choice, William.' Steve's words were ringing in William's ears as he walked towards his luxury cars parked on the drive ahead of him. The buzz of status they had once given him seemed to have faded, no longer filling the emptiness that he felt inside. Still in a daze, he fumbled for his key and opened the front door. Rebecca was still up, sitting in the lounge. As William appeared through the door, she noticed how white he was, the colour completely drained from his face.

Without a word, she opened her arms and gave him a big hug. Rebecca was a wise woman and while she didn't yet know what had happened, she had sensed something brewing for a while. It was clear something was seriously wrong. They could talk later; right now she just wanted to let her husband know he was very dearly loved. As Rebecca wrapped him in her arms, William's body started to tremble again as he struggled to maintain his composure. He clung on rigid, fighting back the urge to cry as he gulped, humiliated. He was surprised to find his body caving in, surrendering. That part of him that always held on tight, holding it all together had lost control. His eyes welled up with tears and he broke down in Rebecca's arms.

'It's okay, darling, it will all be alright – just let it out.' William never cried, he had always been taught to hold his emotion in and put on a brave face, but he felt safe in Rebecca's arms and he couldn't have stopped the tears if he'd tried.

Rebecca gently held William until he was ready to talk. She made them both a cup of tea and settled back on the sofa to listen to what he had to say.

2

Hitting Crisis Point

Once William had regained some composure, he filled Rebecca in on the antics of the evening, and how ashamed he felt for letting everyone down, including himself.

'What am I even doing this job for, Rebecca? I thought I knew … I used to love my work. I've done everything asked of me and achieved great results and exceeded expectations, but now I've totally blown it!'

Rebecca certainly didn't admonish William's achievements. She admired him, and the lifestyle he provided for her and their children was incredible. They had a beautiful home, a holiday retreat in Spain, and Annabel and Tom attended the best private school in the area.

'It's getting tougher,' William continued. 'We're being pushed harder and harder. There are more changes on the way at work and, well, the demands being placed on me … I am struggling to cope. I'm holding my team together by a thread.'

'I am sorry I haven't made enough time for you and the kids. And what's the point of having a gym membership – I haven't been in months.'

Rebecca listened intently as William shared his concerns, she was glad to see him opening up.

'I have neglected you and in some ways have taken you for granted especially with the kids. I know I have let you down as a husband and the kids as their father. And I'm definitely not a good son. My parents are in their 70s and I've hardly seen them in the last year.' Rebecca had never seen William like this before. It was obvious to her that he'd been overdoing it. Finally her gorgeous husband had recognized it too … finally. William seemed to bear the weight of the world on his shoulders. The worries and fears he'd pent up inside for so long were finally being expressed. She felt hugely relieved.

'It's ironic that I was asked to present the Rising Star award as a previous winner, and yet look at me now – a disaster! And my greatest failing has been my neglect of my family.'

Such a thought had never crossed Rebecca's mind and she wanted to reassure William, but it didn't feel right to interrupt just yet, so she just squeezed his hand tight and let him continue.

'Thank you.' He acknowledged her loving gesture.

'I'm glad at least that I have managed to provide for you all. However, it's not worth anything if I make myself ill, lose you along the way and fail to spend any quality time with Annabel and Tom.'

William glanced at a family photo, perched on their mahogany sideboard. It was one of them all laughing at the beach, taken a good few years earlier. They all looked so happy back then, like some bygone idyllic era; he couldn't even remember the last time he had laughed, like really laughed.

'I've done all this to feel secure, to provide for us as a family and get the recognition that goes with it. But in reality, I feel like a sham – an absent husband and father, a total failure. I sometimes wonder why you are still with me?'

'You're not a failure and I'm here because I love you.' Rebecca couldn't hold her silence any longer. 'And everything that's happening is for the best, William. You may not think so now, but trust me, it is.'

'I don't see how any of this could possibly be for the best right now. Steve said something similar to me earlier and I know you're both trying to make me feel better, but it just doesn't make sense. I don't see it!'

'I love you, we're a team, and we will get through this.' And with that Rebecca decided to say no more. Time would tell, of course, and perhaps it was a little premature to pre-empt how he would look back on this moment and be grateful it had happened. She'd seen so many friends live through similar transitions, either with their husbands' careers, or in their own work life. Rebecca had chosen to give up her career when Annabel was born, yet lots of her friends had continued working when they'd started a family. Sometimes she was privately envious hearing about their achievements and opportunities, yet right in this moment she felt extremely thankful to have been just an impartial observer. And even though Rebecca was feeling low herself, when anything happened to her family, she was always there to offer her unwavering support and unconditional love.

It was now 3am and Rebecca suggested they go to bed and talk afresh in the morning. William nodded, unsure he'd be able to sleep, but well aware Rebecca needed some rest as she had to rise early and drive Annabel to an event.

William tossed and turned as the questions endlessly revolved in his mind. How had he managed to let things go so wrong? Why didn't he enjoy his job anymore or get satisfaction from climbing the career ladder like before? Work used to be a pleasure and he'd found fulfilment by developing his team, rising to new challenges and thinking of innovative ways to overcome problems. William loved his job back then, but right now there seemed to be more pressure, changes and demands than ever before. Nothing felt right any more and he couldn't work out how to fix it.

Would he be better off leaving Gant Foster? After all, he was the only one of his close circle of friends who had been with an organization for more than ten years – the others had changed three or four times and were always telling him to broaden his horizons and try something different. Maybe they were right, but then were they all genuinely happy? He wasn't so sure. On the rare occasion they all got together for a Friday night beer there was always someone complaining about work. Better the devil you know, he thought. Perhaps Gant Foster wasn't so bad? The decision over whether to venture on to pastures new or stay put had long been a dilemma. He certainly wanted a change.

Everyone in William's team was quietly worried about what would happen next. Would there be higher targets to hit and more budget cuts to endure? And what if the worst was to happen and they did lose their jobs? Their only option was to knuckle down, continue to work late and take the pressure from William. Whilst in turn, William did the same for Eric. Everyone was tired, physically and mentally – surely things couldn't go on like this for much longer?

Something needed to change, but there was never time for considered thought or focus. In reality he had no time for anything but his career. Relax? Not a chance. Work was always on his mind and the thought of stopping to reflect terrified him. What would that uncover? What would self-questioning reveal? William didn't want to go there, at least not now anyway, and it was the last thing he needed right now. So for the time being he would soldier on as before.

* * *

Beep beep – beep beep – beep beep. It was already 6am and William's alarm burst into life a little too quickly after a couple of hours of disjointed sleep. He hit the snooze button.

19

Beep beep – beep beep – beep beep. Those extra 10 minutes seemed to pass so quickly, but this time William forced himself up, despite the groggy feeling inside his head. He clambered out of bed to get ready for the office.

Rebecca stirred beside him. 'Surely you're not going in today?' She asked sleepily. 'You've hardly slept, you need to rest.'

'I have to, the team needs me and besides I've had a message from Eric requesting to see me at 9am. Anyway, if I don't go in today it would only make the whole thing ten times worse. I'm not going to hide!'

Rebecca sat up, a little more awake. 'Darling, this could be your opportunity to look at life in a new way and make changes based on what you told me last night.'

William sighed. 'Obviously I wasn't thinking straight. It was just an unfortunate incident – these things happen. I guess I just need to get over it somehow.'

Rebecca was frustrated. She'd been so very patient with William and was really hoping this would be the start of him doing things differently, but now she wasn't so sure.

'William, for goodness sake, listen!' Rebecca was tired and irritable. 'Will you please take on board what's happened. I'm fed up of this "macho" behaviour.'

But her words fell on deaf ears, as William rushed out the door. He was on auto-pilot. Rebecca hurriedly got ready to take Annabel to her swimming event.

William's mind was preoccupied as he drove to the office. Every day seemed to merge with the next and he didn't know if he was coming or going, so it was hardly surprising that he'd messed up. Surely there had to be another way – but what and how? He had his job to do, expectations and deadlines to meet and a team to motivate and support. He doubted he did any of these things that well … he just couldn't see the wood for the trees. Whenever a project was finished or a target had been met, there was a period of relief, a celebration and the chance for the team to relax. But the cycle would start over soon enough and everyone would be back in the pressure zone … it was relentless. Yet strangely, accepted.

So it appeared the only way out was to leave, and this was an option William had been exploring, after recently being approached by a headhunter. This seemed even more appealing to him now. He'd been wondering if a new job really might be better for him. He'd go in with a clean slate and a fresh reputation … but what about proving himself to his new colleagues … could he really put himself through that all over again?

He pondered some of the things Steve had said the previous evening. Did he really have a choice? Could things be different?

It was certainly something he'd like to explore, and he made a mental note to invite Steve out for a drink later in the week to talk it through. In the meantime he had to focus on the quarterly results. He walked down the corridor towards Eric's office, took a deep breath, and knocked on his door.

'Good morning, William,' said Eric, as William sheepishly sidled in. 'You don't look so great today. Take a seat. Coffee?'

William nodded gratefully, welcoming a caffeine fix.

Eric buzzed Serena, his highly efficient PA, asking her to bring in the drinks. While they waited, he opened up the conversation.

'Well, I think we both know why you're not looking so great, and why I've asked you here this morning.'

William took a long deep breath and waited for Eric to continue.

'I'm guessing you didn't sleep well after the awards dinner?'

William was grateful Eric had started the dialogue as he hadn't a clue where to begin. At least he now had an opportunity to respond.

'I'm so sorry Eric, I let you and Jason down. I let myself down. I was very grateful you chose me to present the award and I blew it – especially after the way you introduced me, which I truly appreciated. I just lost my thread I guess.'

'It certainly wasn't your finest hour, that's for sure,' said Eric, a playful hint of sarcasm in his voice. 'But it's happened and we can't change that,' he smiled. Eric was wise enough not to ask William how he was feeling. It was obvious and that line of questioning wouldn't help; or was it that Eric was afraid to ask this question? Maybe he didn't know how to handle the response or accept that it would be good for William to get things off his chest.

By now the lack of sleep, upset and caffeine were making William think irrationally. 'Listen, Eric, I'll totally understand if you want to fire me.'

'Why on earth would I do that?' Eric stared at him bemused, with a trace of a smile. 'Okay, you made a complete hash of your presentation last night, but otherwise you're still an asset to Gant Foster.'

William cringed. While Eric's direct approach was refreshing, it was painful to be reminded of his on stage fiasco.

'But let's talk about it, while it's still fresh,' continued Eric.

Raw more like, thought William.

'We all have our moments in our careers, William. Looking back over mine, some of the hardest knocks have been my biggest learnings, even though they didn't feel like it at the time.'

Eric was actually thinking about his divorce, but wasn't ready to share that story with William or with anyone for that matter. It may have been three years ago, but it still felt like yesterday and the pain hadn't subsided. His entire focus these days was on retiring so he could have a better quality of life. He desperately wished he'd done things differently in his marriage and could see William heading the same way if he wasn't careful.

'I'm sure this will play on your mind for a while, William, but what have you learned from everything that's been happening?'

The question caught William by surprise and he was surprised by Eric's keenness to get straight to the point. Okay, he could be direct, even a little matter-of-fact at times, but he wouldn't usually dive in like this. Not that William minded; he was relieved his boss was showing some empathy and understanding, rather than dwelling on the negatives to make him feel worse than he already did.

'To be honest, Eric, I thought on it last night and I'm still really confused and embarrassed by the whole episode. I had made the speech all about me, and as I listened to Melissa, I realized how shortsighted I had been. As Melissa spoke, I came to my senses, and realized I had nothing else to say. Eric, in truth I think I have been totally overstressed and it's taking its toll. People are saying I should view this episode as a gift, a wonderful opportunity to change. I did have an interesting conversation with Steve as he drove me home. He explained the destructive impact his overworking and tendency to be too driven had on his health and wellbeing.'

Eric was well aware of what had happened to Steve and actually felt a little guilty – all the more reason to have this chat with

24

William, he thought. With Eric it had been his divorce, with Steve, his health, and he certainly didn't want William to experience either of those scenarios – or worse.

'Okay, so what impact has all of this had on you?' asked Eric.

'I'm concerned that I could be heading the same way as him, if I am not careful. I'm so tired and stressed and feel like all the days are blurred into one and that I'm on a never-ending treadmill. I have to keep going … I'm too scared of what would happen if I stopped. This situation is really making me think. Bad things always happen to someone else and we think we're immune – that it won't happen to us. Don't get me wrong, I was sympathetic about Steve's heart attack, but hadn't considered it could actually happen to me. And because I've been feeling so stressed and worn out myself, it hit home.'

Eric took a sip of his coffee, sat back in his chair and encouraged William to continue. 'Go on,' he said, without hesitating. 'What else?'

'I've not mentioned this before, but I had a shock a few years ago when my father had a stroke just three months after he'd retired. It was a really worrying time for our family, but fortunately he pulled through.'

William paused as he thought about spending more time with his parents – something he vowed to do while his father was recovering. But his old habits had kicked back in and the visits began to dry up.

'I seem to keep getting these reminders, and I need to take stock.'

Instinctively there was a part of William that knew life was giving him these messages for a reason and he'd been continually ignoring them. This internal voice seemed to be repeatedly asking if he was going to wait until something terrible happened to him before he faced up to things. Or maybe someone else's wake up call would serve to wake him up too!

Reassured that William was sufficiently concerned about the trajectory he was on, Eric softened his approach a little. 'Are you spending much time with Rebecca and the kids?' he enquired. 'Annabel must be getting ready for her exams now? And Tom, is he still into his music?'

This last question really stopped William in his tracks and made him feel guilty. Sure he occasionally helped with their homework, but didn't really spend much quality time with either of them. He'd usually arrive home late, collapse in a chair and start ruminating on some problem back at Gant Foster. Even on holiday, he would be constantly checking his emails, as if the world would stop if he disconnected from the internet. Every day William would call the office from the balcony overlooking the pool of their holiday home to make sure his team members were okay. He didn't need to of course, it was simply his need to feel secure and in control. And he often wondered what it would be like to go on holiday without getting ill. He'd usually get a cold the minute he stopped working, and on one occasion earlier in the year he'd spent the whole of the first week of a ten-day break in bed, ill and exhausted, leaving

Rebecca to entertain Annabel and Tom on her own, which was hardly fair on her.

William answered honestly, he felt he had nothing to lose by being open and it was rare for Eric to be in listening mode. 'No, not nearly as much as I'd like because of the pressures we are under here. Annabel is studying most of the time and I would love to help her more and Tom, yes, he loves his piano, but I really screwed up last week, because I was so caught up in everything that I missed his concert.'

Eric felt bad about this. He'd stepped back a little because of his own situation and let Steve and William take more responsibility, which they were more than capable of doing. But, clearly he didn't want them to be getting ill or burnt out, nor did he want their marriages or home lives to suffer. Deep down, Eric did care and wanted the best for, and out of, the people working for him – it was vital they were fit and healthy or there would be a negative knock-on for Gant Foster. It had happened to Steve with his health, so he had to support William – he relied on him playing his part in the business too much. Eric promised himself that he, too, would become more aware of what was happening around him and make some changes. This was partly why he hadn't been as hard on William as he could have been. He'd been angry during the awards dinner for sure, because William's disastrous speech affected his own reputation, but he'd slept on it and regained some perspective. Eric needed William in the business more than he knew. So it seemed there were learnings and wake up calls for everyone, mused Eric.

'Steve mentioned he had a coach,' said William. 'Apparently the company helped him secure her services and I'm intrigued to know if this is something that could help me too.'

'That's right, he's working with Susannah Lockwood – she used to be the Director of Organizational Effectiveness at McKnight Marshall. Apparently she has a unique way of combining coaching with mentoring to get the best results; I have heard great things about her.'

William was intrigued. Steve hadn't mentioned that little detail, but then to be fair, he hadn't really been in the space to take in the details last night. McKnight Marshall was a world-renowned and respected consultancy, which made him feel quite nervous. Still, he'd come this far and approached Eric, so he would carry on exploring if this could be a worthwhile option for him.

Although Eric had felt reservations at first, he'd seen a big improvement in Steve and knew plenty of senior executives who had a coach; it seemed to be an accepted practice. And the benefits he had observed from afar in Steve, and consequently, within his team, had already more than outweighed the investment in hiring Susannah. While it was clearly working for Steve, Eric wasn't ready to 'go there' himself because he was afraid of what he might have to face. He was, however, more than willing to support William if coaching would keep him at Gant Foster. He certainly couldn't risk losing him, which would only bring more pressure on himself.

'Why don't you have another chat with Steve and get an introduction?' suggested Eric. 'I'm happy to support you if you think it will help.'

'Thanks, Eric, I will, I want to understand how it works first; this is all new to me.'

With that, Eric closed their meeting. 'Okay, William, just let me know what you decide and if I can be of any further help just let me know and keep your head up.'

'Thanks again, Eric, I'll do my best,' said William, inwardly fretting how he was going to survive it. The meeting with Eric had gone much better than he'd expected, so that at least was a good start.

As the door closed behind William, Eric reclined in his chair. While he'd hopefully made William think, he'd also given himself plenty to reflect on. Perhaps he'd benefit from a coaching session with Susannah himself some day, he thought. When the time was right …

3

A Long Lunch

William cringed whenever he thought about the awards ceremony, but the subsequent realization that it was possible to do things differently was a comfort, even if he didn't know yet what that looked like. The prospect of change felt strange, yet exciting at the same time. What might the future look like, he wondered?

The first opportunity to see Steve was at lunchtime. William had passed by his office several times that morning hoping to thank him and invite him out for a drink after work one evening, to find out a little more about the coaching he'd mentioned. Every time he had glanced through the slatted window blinds he could see Steve engrossed in a meeting with a woman he didn't recognize, but now on his way back from a meeting he noticed she had just left Steve's office and was walking away down the corridor.

'Hey William, I've just finished a great coaching session with Susannah Lockwood,' said Steve, looking happy and relaxed, as William entered his office.

Steve beckoned William to take a seat on the leather chair opposite his desk…'I'm so impressed with how much Susannah's coaching has helped me,' said Steve, 'since … well, you know … since I returned to work after being so unwell.'

'I hadn't realized things still weren't working for you, Steve. I thought you'd bounced back.'

Steve chuckled to himself at the innocence of William's comment, though he couldn't blame him for making it. How was he to know what a profound impact the coaching had made? 'Everything's great – my life is working much better for me now. I'm living and leading in a way that's right for me and I wouldn't have it any other way.'

William was confounded. Was it really possible to turn your life around like this?

'Since working with Susannah I've become aware of what's most important to me. That's how I make my decisions these days and I'm healthier, happier, and far less stressed as a result. I wish I had hired her long before I got ill, then maybe it wouldn't have happened.'

William was quick to put two and two together. It all made sense now … Steve was spending fewer hours in the office, yet was more productive than ever before. The coaching was clearly having a positive effect.

'You know what I was like before,' said Steve. 'I spent virtually my entire life behind this desk, but now I can't tell you how much

I'm enjoying spending more quality time with Michelle and our boys. I feel much more in control and to know I have the power of choice in all areas of my life is truly liberating. I've never felt better.'

William was pleased to hear Steve talking like this. They'd been friends since his first week at Gant Foster and he delighted in seeing him happy and content after struggling for so long. And for him to keep mentioning 'choice', well, that was a revelation. Could you always have a choice? William was curious and pressed Steve to tell him more.

'Coaching isn't simply about making things right, in fact far from it. It helps you operate from your true potential, gain insights to help you grow and become more fulfilled in the process. It's a very positive, forward focused process and I'm doing fewer hours than I used to, yet as a team we've doubled our productivity. It's largely down to the different way I'm leading, a way that works better for me, allowing me to be true to myself and let go of the masks I was wearing – no more pretending, it's truly liberating! At our last weekly meeting they told me they're thriving in this new environment of trust, support and respect. And, you know, William, it's actually quite natural once you empower and engage people and learn to let go of how things "should" be done. But first, you have to start with yourself. It's only more recently that I have started to have this impact on my team as well, and now it's almost becoming second nature.'

'I tell you what,' said Steve purposefully. 'I'm just off for a lunchtime walk by the river – why don't you come with me and we can chat and get something to eat?'

'Sorry, Steve, I'd love to but I really haven't got time right now. I've got so much to do – you know what it's like.'

'Yes, I know what it *used* to be like,' said Steve. 'But things are different for me now and they could be for you too – I thought you wanted to do things differently?'

'I do, I do … Okay, I get your point!'

'Good, then go get your jacket. There is no time like the present!'

Back in his own office William watched as his personal assistant, Lynne, neatly placed some files into his office cabinet, before turning to face him.

'I'm going for a walk and some lunch with Steve – I shouldn't be longer than an hour.'

'No problem, I've got everything covered here,' she said reassuringly. 'Take as long as you need.'

William was puzzled by Lynne's relaxed reaction. It suddenly occurred to William that everyone else seemed to know something he didn't! Steve, Rebecca and now Lynne. Even Eric was slightly more mellow than usual. What was going on?

As they walked beside the river, William waited for the right moment to raise the coaching subject again, but he didn't want to interrupt Steve, who was waxing lyrical about all the rediscovered joy he was experiencing from spending time with his family at weekends, and with Michelle on their weekly date nights.

'So you honestly think coaching will benefit me, that it's really worth a try?'

'I most certainly do,' said Steve, pleased that his friend valued his opinion. 'But only if you're open to it … that's the key. I can only speak from personal experience, but doing this inner work has really helped me not just to change a few things, but to really transform.'

That was a big statement to make, thought William. He knew he wanted to make some changes – but transformation? He had no idea what that might even look like, never mind whether it was actually possible!

'Steve, I'm open to it for sure, but wary of what others may think. I mean, I made a right fool of myself at the awards dinner and now don't want to give the impression that I can't stand on my own two feet …'

Steve smiled, but knew William was serious. Misreading the smirk on Steve's face, William pressed on.

'It's not funny, that's how I feel. I don't want to look like a loser.'

'Do you view me as a loser?' asked Steve. 'I don't believe you do, but if you do, I'm okay with that and that's exactly why I recommend you take on a coach; someone like Susannah, because it will really help you let go of caring about what others think! Coaching is a forward-thinking process; the coach will listen carefully to what you're saying and, more importantly, what you're not saying. They will ask you questions that you hadn't even thought of, challenge your thinking and support you in making changes to ultimately become the best you can be. Think about it, William, have you ever heard of a top sport's person, someone who is really at the top of their game, who doesn't have a coach?'

William was still a little uncertain but remained open. 'Now you put it like that, it's making a bit more sense.'

'If you're prepared to work on things and take ownership of the process, you'll do great. Yes, it involves adjusting and correcting your course along the way and it's not always easy. No one expects to get it right all the time, but if you open yourself up to the learning and discovery you'll definitely reap the rewards.'

'You're starting to make it sound intriguing and almost fun,' said William. He couldn't remember the last time he had thought of anything to do with work as fun.

Steve laughed again. 'That's a great way to look at it. It is fun, but be aware you'll also have to face some stuff that's not easy. You may not want to face the reality of certain things, but my advice is to keep going with the process and stick with it. That way, you'll make lasting changes in your life.'

'I had no idea that you were doing all this, Steve, and I'm sorry for not noticing. I knew you were taking it easier since your health scare, but the last 24 hours has opened my eyes to just how differently you're doing things.'

Steve was unruffled. 'No worries. Most people haven't noticed and that's probably because they're too wrapped up in their own stuff and will probably only pick up on it if they happen to have a moment of realization like the one you're just reaching. Besides, I'm keeping a low profile. My health is my number one priority and while the doctors have said I'm improving I know there's still a way to go, so I won't be tackling the situation at Gant Foster just yet. Maybe that will be your role, William!'

Steve knew when to stop. He only wanted to sow the seed in William's mind; he didn't want to overwhelm him. As William pondered, Steve turned the focus back to himself.

'This is the first time I've really expressed my truth with anyone other than myself and during my sessions with Susannah.'

'I appreciate you are sharing this with me,' William said, although he did think the term 'expressed my truth' was a bit odd, which Steve picked up on.

'Let me explain what I mean by that. When I say my truth, I'm referring to the story of what happened to me, and more importantly, to who I am and what I stand for. I like the term "expressing my truth" because sometimes we can get stuck in our story and beliefs that don't serve us. When we go to the truth, we draw out the real stuff, straight from the heart.'

William found this 'new age' language intriguing if not a little uncomfortable. It wasn't what he was used to, but rather than dwell on it and try to work it out for himself, he nodded, encouraging Steve to continue, as he could tell this was important to him.

'The further I travel on this journey the more I find out who I really am, not who I was pretending to be. I'm slowly removing the masks I used to wear each day at Gant Foster to reveal my true self. And do you know what, William? One of those masks was the one I wore when I thought I was leading. Actually, let's not call it leading, it wasn't really, it was managing; managing to get through each day.'

'Oh yes, I know that one,' interjected William.

William hadn't expected to be so enthralled by Steve's coaching revelations, and it was reassuring to discover they had so much in common. The more he spoke, the more William could identify.

'I used to think I had authority over others because of my position and the fancy title screwed to my office door,' Steve continued, 'but that's nonsense. I don't have authority over anyone, apart from myself. I can influence and empower others, yes, but have authority? That's just another mask we wear. It boosts our ego and tricks us in having a false sense of some kind of power. The thing is, we do have power, but it's the way we use it that counts. We all have our own personal power, which allows us to take ownership and responsibility for ourselves and ultimately lead more consciously.'

William sipped on his Berry Blast, and was quite enjoying it. And the tuna salad was making a tasty change from the habitual hurried sandwich at his desk. Steve had suggested a new place for lunch, which was part of his new 'looking after himself' routine. William had obliged him and was pleasantly surprised that he was enjoying his healthier lunch.

'What about your heart attack?' William asked tentatively, knowing it must have been linked to the stress Steve had been under.

'I have to take responsibility for that too. I didn't listen to the "nudges" I was getting or see the warning signs. That's why I'm so keen to support you if I can. It's important to be alert to these nudges that life presents us before they become ugly.'

Steve deliberately chose the word 'life' rather than 'the soul', as he didn't want to confuse William. He remembered how it had been for him starting out on his 'inner journey' of discovery and self leadership when some of the associated language had initially taken some adjusting to.

'It's good for you to take some action now, while the event is still raw,' Steve continued.

'Don't remind me,' William cringed again.

'Within these nudges, dramas or traumas, depending on how you perceive them, lie rich opportunities for growth and learning. I'm learning to notice the nudges now and listen to their meaning. They can be faint, almost like a whisper, but in my case it took a steamroller, metaphorically speaking, to get me to stop and listen, because I had ignored the nudges and even some hefty smacks in the face. I would liken yours to a "smack in the face moment", – one that really takes the wind out of your sails. Ignore it at your peril, for then you'll have to deal with the steamroller! That's why I now listen to the nudges, so I can course-correct and hopefully avoid the other two happening.'

Steve wondered whether he was going too fast or deep for William to follow. After all, he'd never shared this with anyone before, not even Michelle. Not because he hadn't wanted to, but because he had been unsure how best to describe it. He had also been a little hesitant over how much to share and didn't want to come across all evangelical, but William seemed keen to know more and Steve's aim was to share just enough for him to see the benefits of having a coach. Steve was in full flow, the words pouring out of him as he tried to help his good friend.

'Your current predicament really reminds me where I was at before I had the heart attack. I see myself in you in so many ways and hopefully I can influence you to make different choices and avoid what I've been through. I really encourage you to change what you're doing and look at the person you're pretending to be. You are likely to discover it isn't who you really are and the discoveries you'll make are rewarding, to say the least.'

While William had been surprised by some of the things Steve had told him after the awards dinner, he was now completely stunned. Here was his friend sitting beside him, pouring his heart out as though he'd been brought back to life and given a second chance.

'Steve, this is all a bit strange for me, but I am interested and if you don't mind me saying, you're talking like you've been reborn or something!'

Steve laughed. 'I love it. Do you know what? That's a perfect description of how I feel! You know me well enough to understand I'd never have spoken to you like this before. I couldn't have been this honest, but now it feels so natural. It's who I am and I'm proud and happy to be rediscovering myself.'

William felt privileged that Steve had opened up to him and his words were starting to make sense.

'I didn't expect to say this, but what you've so openly shared is making quite an impact on me. I appreciate it.'

'That's kind of you to say, William. I want to have an impact on people, but right now, I want to help you. If others are ready to hear what I have to say, I'll happily share it. Some may judge me, but I don't care. I'd drifted away and become disconnected from my truth, William, just like you appear to have done. Maybe one day I'll use what's happened to me to serve others on a wider scale. While I've not yet recovered enough to do that fully within Gant Foster, who knows – perhaps if I can manage to influence your choices and actions, you in turn may come to sway others in the company?'

Did Steve know something he didn't? William wondered, as he had intimated this a couple of times now. William couldn't think about that right now, even though it did resonate at some level.

His main concern was to stop himself heading down the route of burnout or other serious health problems. He was quietly concerned that he had been ignoring his own nudges and a visit to the doctor about those chest pains was long overdue. He would make an appointment this afternoon.

The penny had dropped for William. Steve had slowed down and everyone thought it was because of his heart attack. Of course that was partly true and that's what people would expect. Yet the reason he'd not shared his learnings is because no one would listen to him. It was obvious to William now – people aren't generally ready to listen until they've had some kind of mid-life crisis or a poignant moment of realization. If only people acted on their nudges as they happened and saved themselves from the harsher smacks in the face … or even those dreaded steamrollers of life. How different life would be!

'The process Susannah is taking me through has helped me discover my motivations, my drivers and what's really important,' Steve continued. 'And they aren't what I thought they would be, but it's given me a deeper clarity and I now understand why I do the things I do. Before my heart attack, my behaviour wasn't in line with who I was at my core, which is why I felt drained, overwhelmed and restless. I am still in the process of getting to know myself and I am really beginning to be the real me. It changes everything!'

Steve had mentioned the 'restless' word again and William was quick to pick up on it. 'That's exactly how I feel, Steve – restless.'

'Brilliant!' exclaimed Steve, so vehemently that several people in the cafe turned to stare at him.

'Brilliant … why brilliant?' Wondered William, and then pressing his palm to his forehead as the penny dropped. 'Ah yes – it's an opportunity to change something!'

'Yes, William.' Steve smiled. 'You're getting it! It is likely your soul is restless, because it wants you to listen and make some changes. It knows there's another way and that you've been ignoring its nudges. The same thing happened with me, but it took a heart attack to make me take notice.'

'I think I'm getting this now,' William grinned. 'Being restless is a good thing?'

'Absolutely! And for so many reasons.' Steve was delighted that William was getting this. 'It could be to make you stop and listen, to give you courage to take the next step, or even to stop you from going stale. I recommend you embrace it, because there'll come a point when it gets so frustrating that you'll reach breaking point and either have a health scare, like me, or suffer some other traumatic consequence. Have you considered that your "experience" at the awards dinner was an indication of this?'

William cringed again as he recalled his stuttering speech. 'Yes of course, as you've explained things, but my experience surely pales into insignificance compared to a major health scare?'

43

'It's all relative, William; it's how it makes you feel that matters,' said Steve. 'This is partly why I keep bringing the subject up, when I know you want to hide from it, but getting you to go there, to relive it again, can be good leverage.'

'Oh can it now?' William responded a little sarcastically to make light of it. 'Well you've certainly got leverage,' he sighed, with a smile of surrender. 'Count me in!'

'Great! This is a good place from which to make the conscious choice to take action and turn things around. Consider your own health. I mean, you're exhausted and not thinking straight. I don't want to alarm you, but that's how I was before I got ill.'

William had noticed how Steve had been really overdoing it before his heart attack. He had accepted more and more work and never switched off, preferring to do things himself rather than delegate or put on other people.

'There was a lot of pressure,' explained Steve. 'I thought my job would be on the line if I wasn't seen to be going the extra mile. In reality, though I didn't know it back then, I was operating from a place of fear, not courage, and this almost cost me my health, not to mention my life. That heart attack was a major wake up call, but having taken a step back and started some inner work, I can now see it in perspective. I consider myself lucky. I've survived and realize the lessons and learnings were an invaluable gift which would probably have passed me by had this not happened.

So many people are operating from a place of fear and sooner or later this has to have an impact.'

William was fascinated. Steve was so knowledgeable about it all and seemed to have everything figured out.

'Trust me, William, it's all too easy when something has passed, to forget the intensity of it and kid yourself that everything's okay again. But if you don't act now, something else will happen and it seems your soul really wants you to listen this time. I don't want to scare you, but if you don't, it's likely something bigger and more alarming will rear up. Think back, what nudges have you let pass before?'

Now that William knew what he was looking for, he could think of quite a few, but the most obvious was his father's stroke just after he had retired. He'd worked hard all his life and then got ill. He also recognized the same 'work hard' patterns in himself. The health issue nudges were certainly showing up around him, in Steve and with his dad. These further highlighted the occasional chest pains William had been experiencing and too readily ignoring. They didn't feel like anything major, but he kept promising himself he would get them checked when he had more time.

Then there was the situation with Russell, a member of his team, which he had been continually putting off. Russell frequently spoke out inappropriately in team meetings, which William had turned a blind eye to, hoping Russell would eventually let up. This was one of many things that were challenging his leadership style, and which he was aware, needed addressing. He had also heard an interview on the radio recently about the benefits of being more bold and courageous – a topic he had also read about in a recent business magazine article. William was also becoming aware of a sort of 'inner voice' that seemed to be urging – 'just be yourself' … but this had just confused him – for just who was he being, if not himself?

Steve sensed William's mood drop and stayed silent, allowing him to process his thoughts. From his own experience he knew not to interrupt, even though it was difficult not to jump in and try to make it all okay. Feeling the pain was an important part of this process, as he had learned only too well. Fortunately there was a way through it.

When Steve did speak again, his voice was full of compassion. 'It's okay, William, it hurts doesn't it, when you think back; I understand. It's the things we bring into consciousness over time that make us pay attention to the nudges. How are you doing? Perhaps that's enough for one day.'

William looked away and gazed out of the window. The conversation was making him feel a little uncomfortable and embarrassed now, but Steve was supporting him and he didn't just want to brush it off. He took a deep breath. 'You're right Steve, I've known for a while that there's a part of me wanting to be someone different, a part that wants to do something more meaningful I guess, but I have always just brushed it off as I didn't have a clue where to start.'

Nodding his head, Steve agreed saying 'Yes, I get that, truly I do. That's the shift I am going through at the moment and why Susannah is much better placed than me to take you through this. It all starts with discovering who you are at your core and finding out what is truly important to you, knowing and living your own core values. It was eye-opening for me when I really understood this.'

'I like to think I'm a good, honest man,' said William, now allowing himself a boost. 'Rebecca says I'm a decent husband, father and son. I accept I could spend more time with my family, but they know how much I love them and I do always try to do the right thing – are these the sort of things you mean, my family values?'

'There's more to it than that. It seems a lot of people think they know their core values, but when you truly discover what they are and the power they hold, they totally transform the way you show up. They are our "inner compass" and impact all our decisions, our relationships and communications and the goals and intentions we set and achieve – or fail to achieve, whichever the case may be.'

'Ah, well perhaps I don't know what my core values are then,' conceded William.

Steve grinned. 'You're not alone, few people do. Some think they do, but it's rarely the case. I certainly didn't. Identifying your core values takes some working out. They're the things that matter most to us in life and yet we generally don't spend the time on them that they deserve. It's likely there's a disconnect between who you are at your core and how you are showing up right now, hence the restless feeling. Can I have permission to challenge you, William?'

William laughed. 'What, you don't think I've been challenged enough this last 24 hours? Yes, keep going.' William was surprisingly alert considering he'd been on an emotional rollercoaster ride.

'Let's look at a couple of things you said there, describing your-self as "a good honest man" and someone who "does the right thing". I've no doubt you think you are, but I suspect you're not being completely honest with yourself right now, are you? Do you really always do the right thing? For who? Yourself? Your team? Your family? I'm not so sure I've seen that happening, William. Do you even know what the right thing is for you? A loving husband, father and son? I'm not here to doubt that at all, but are those people getting the benefit of your love, your presence and your time?'

Steve's words knocked William for six. He'd never heard him speak in such a forthright way before and Steve wasn't about to apologize.

'Most people are just bumbling along like I used to, and how you were until now, William. They don't see what's missing until it smacks them in the face. This is why you feel disconnected and restless – you're not being true to yourself. It seems, like me, you've drifted along complacently for too long and perhaps lost sight of who you really are. Maybe you're hiding from your true self – the real you.'

Steve had really made William think. How was he supposed to know who he was when he had lost all sense of what was important?

'I've got so much to do … the budgets, the quarterly report, managing my team. I can't see the wood for the trees, but I have to keep going.'

'That's just your ego talking and those things are insignificant if you don't have your health.'

William looked confused.

'I really would encourage you to listen to your intuition more. That part of you that knows things can be different. It seems you've had several nudges already, William … you have to decide whether you're ready to step up. This is your moment to get to know yourself better, make changes … experience a transformation even!'

Steve certainly seemed to be acting differently and was surer of himself than ever before. Maybe it wasn't just because of the heart attack that he was behaving more calmly. Was this his new way of being? Steve seemed to be advocating a deeper approach of going inside and becoming more aware of who he was before making changes on the outside for all to see.

Steve sensed he may have pushed William enough and his intention was purely to sow some seeds and encourage him to hire a coach, so he thought he would check. 'Is this a bit much for you,

William? I'm not sure how I would have responded to all this heavy talk from someone other than a coach, prior to me working with a coach myself.'

'No, really it's fine,' William smiled thoughtfully. 'I'm just reflecting on what you are saying. A lot of it is hitting home.'

'Before we can genuinely support and provide for other people, we should help ourselves first … It's certainly not selfish to focus on yourself. Let's face it; can we be of any real use to anyone if we're "suffering" as a result? Think of it like this – if you're on a plane and the oxygen masks drop down, whose would you put on first?'

'My own of course.'

'Exactly, you would need to give yourself oxygen before you can help others.'

William couldn't disagree with that. It was obvious Steve had prioritized his own health and wellbeing and William was beginning to realize he'd have to work on himself first too. He loved helping people and was eager to ensure he didn't let Eric and the team down, but not if it was to the detriment of his health and his family.

'My advice would be to embrace it, William. It's exciting and you may even find you have a deeper purpose; or perhaps an exciting and compelling vision for your future will emerge, who knows!'

Even though William didn't fully understand everything Steve was telling him, he was beginning to get a good feeling about this. Could it really work for him? And the way Steve spoke was drawing him in – his tone was relaxed and the words convincing. William had never heard him talk like this before … his words seemed to resonate deep inside, calling him to take action.

'I'd highly recommend meeting Susannah for a chat. She is the expert and can explain this so much better than me. I just wanted to share enough to give you an idea of what it could be like. Susannah is supportive, impartial and doesn't judge, but wise enough to know when to challenge and ask questions – some of which might be quite direct. But that's what will lead you to access the discoveries, insights and awareness that will help you make the important decisions.'

Steve realized he was giving too much information. He didn't want to add to William's overwhelm, but was glad he'd been able to spot the warning signs and step in.

'William, this is your journey and I don't want to interfere, but I'm here for you if you need me, you only need to ask. Besides, I'm still facing up to my own challenges and focusing on my world. It's taking a lot of courage to make these changes and not worry about what people think, especially now I've stopped staying late at the office and taking work home. I'm sure people are making allowances and expect me to return to my old ways once I'm back to full health and vitality, but I intend to carry on this new balanced lifestyle. I love swimming each morning and taking an early evening walk – I feel calmer and more relaxed than ever and I'm not giving that up.'

Steve knew William would need plenty of courage to stop conforming, but if he could extricate himself from the expectations of others, William would be free to step fully into his leadership power and bring about positive change at Gant Foster. Steve saw a lot of potential in his friend, probably more than William could see in himself. He'd shared his experience and offered some insights. It was now up to William to take this on board.

'So, Steve, tell me a little more about Susannah – what kind of questions will she ask? Has she been through this experience of restlessness herself?'

'I think you've endured quite enough for one lunch break,' smiled Steve, glancing at his watch and realizing they'd been out of the office for nearly two hours. 'What I will say, though, is she'll ask you some very powerful questions to make you stop and think deeper and differently. Susannah's a great listener. She'll hear what you say and also work with you intuitively, and although at times it may be uncomfortable, that's how you'll ultimately make the breakthroughs.'

William's concentration had broken and reality kicked in. He could ill afford to be away from his desk for this long and he was desperate to get back. He pushed back his seat and hurriedly poked his arms into the sleeves of his jacket.

'Hey, slow down! Lynne said she had everything covered.'

William was already heading for the door, mumbling something about being short staffed and preparing for tomorrow's call with the US office.

'Hey, wait for me!' Steve paid the bill and adjusted his stride to keep up with William who was now in full panic mode.

'Sorry, Steve, I have to get back … there's so much to do. I don't want to appear ungrateful. I am truly thankful for your time and all that you have shared, it's really helped me a lot.'

'Don't be sorry, William. Just take a moment to recognize that for the last couple of hours you've taken some valuable time out for you – congratulations! It's not only important, but essential. Try to breathe a little and calm yourself if you can … you'll be of much more benefit to everyone that way.'

William knew Steve was right. There was no point flapping as soon as he got back to the office. 'Thanks again, I am going to give the coaching a go – if it's working for you then I'm hopeful it can help me too.'

4

Will You Go There?

At Eric's recommendation, William arranged to meet with Susannah for an initial discussion, prior to formally beginning any coaching, to make sure they both felt comfortable working together.

Susannah asked some helpful questions to find out where he was currently at and whether he was ready and willing to look at himself and make the necessary changes. She explained how the process would work and warned William that it would take him out of his comfort zone.

'It may not be easy and it will probably feel painful at times,' Susannah said. 'Are you prepared to go there William?' And her words would stick in his mind in the days that followed. 'Do I have permission to challenge you and ask questions you may never have been asked before? It's likely we'll go to places that are uncomfortable for you, but with my support it will help bring about the changes you desire and embed them as new practices in your daily life.'

Following the meeting, Susannah sent William a questionnaire, asking him to complete it before their first session. The questions forced him to think differently and some of them stumped him, such as one that inquired, 'Define what success means to you.' William had never asked himself that before and as he automatically typed out a list of his most prized material possessions, he paused to reflect. 'I already have most of these things, I'm well up the career ladder and my kids are in private education, yet I'm still not happy. In fact, I'm fed up and exhausted! Is it possible that success can mean something different? Does the material value of my possessions really define success? He wondered, quickly realizing the absurdity of ever having believed that it could.

Susannah had assured William the questionnaire was just the starting point … to get him thinking and 'in the zone' for their sessions and that it also gave her a deeper idea of where he was at, what he wanted to gain from the coaching and an indication of whether they could work on this together. 'I have to make sure you're committed to this process,' she'd told him. 'And you'll have to do some work in between sessions too if this is going to work properly.'

Going through the questions, William was nervous and excited in equal measure. And though he didn't really know what to expect, having discussed the bigger picture and what might be possible, he was pleased to be doing something positive at last. During their initial discussion, Susannah had helped William identify the following key areas of focus and desired outcomes for his coaching sessions:

Be a more courageous and confident leader

William had shared how he felt like he was barely managing, let alone leading. One example he gave Susannah for this was his difficulty in handling one of the members of his team, namely Russell. Russell's cynicism was having a negative impact on the team, which he could do without. William explained how powerless he felt to tackle this issue head on.

Embrace the restless feeling

Susannah suggested to William how by shifting his initial desire to overcome his restlessness, he could learn to embrace it instead. He could use it to tune into what was most important to him. Susannah knew that ultimately his restlessness would become his greatest teacher. She would let William discover this for himself.

Finding more balance

William had a real sense of being out of balance – in his health, in his leadership style, and in the time he spent at work in proportion to that spent at home. He was eager to attain greater clarity in this area, and particularly keen to create more time for his family. He just wasn't sure which work responsibilities if any he could offload to achieve this. He wanted to make changes, and he had to start somewhere.

'I've been feeling restless and stuck, Susannah,' William explained. 'I've lost direction and a meaning for why I am doing what I am doing. I know something's missing in my life, though I'm not sure what.'

57

'Embrace your restlessness, William,' encouraged Susannah. 'It's good to acknowledge that you know something is missing or that maybe there is a deeper reason or purpose, but let's hold that lightly for now. What I'm about to say may not make much sense right now, but it will as the process unfolds. I'm going to invite you to look deep within, to get to who you truly are at the core, and you can decide later if you wish to use what you discover in your own life to empower and influence others, or if this is indeed part of a bigger purpose – let's see what unfolds for you. It all starts with self-leadership and it will require courage and some "out of comfort zone moments". Will you go there?'

William smiled and nodded. 'Yes, I will go there, for sure, I have to. Let's do this!' And at that moment Susannah knew she had his commitment. She could help him.

'You'll have to be patient, William. All of this will be explored over a series of coaching sessions and the momentum will gather as you experience new awarenesses about yourself. The first thing you're going to discover, or perhaps rediscover, are your core values. Once you've really clarified your values, you'll have a solid foundation and be better equipped to make conscious decisions, ones that you absolutely know are right for you. And from there you'll build more effective relationships, experience much better communications and set goals and objectives that are in alignment with what is truly important to you.'

William was impressed. 'I've never thought too much about my purpose'. Was it possible to find deeper meaning in his career?

'Don't worry too much about that just yet,' said Susannah. 'Trust the process and we'll get to that soon enough. We'll spend our first two sessions discovering your values – the things that matter most to you, that motivate you and drive your decisions and behaviour. This will then set the foundation for everything else to follow.'

William hadn't given much considered thought to his values though Steve had certainly sparked his interest in the potential of doing so. He couldn't really think beyond family values at this juncture. He knew that integrity and being honest were important to him, but what other values guided his life? He was open to the process and found he naturally felt safe with Susannah. He had a good feeling about the sessions and felt ready to give them a go.

William was definitely ready to *go there*, wherever *there* might be.

ARE YOU READY TO 'GO THERE?'

This is the first of a series of exercises, which you will find at the end of each chapter starting from this one, Chapter 4, onwards. The purpose is to help you discover who you truly are at your core and support you to lead with courage from this place. I invite you to work through the questions in a sequential order initially, as they follow William's transformation from a Restless Executive to a Courageous Leader. The questions have been designed to build on each other, leading you towards your own transformation should you chose to embrace your restlessness and 'go there'.

Your Discovery Questions

As you read these questions, allow your intuition to guide your answers.

1. *Have you experienced a moment of realization? What impact did it have on you?*

2. *How do you recognize restlessness in yourself?*

3. *What nudges are you acting on or ignoring?*

4. *What are you questioning about yourself?*

5. *Where are you not being true to yourself?*

6. *What does your soul want you to know?*

7. *What is the gift in your restlessness?*

PART 2

The Discovery

'Your core values are at the heart of every decision you make, every relationship you encounter and every goal you achieve, whether you are consciously aware of it or not.'

5

Values Discovery

Susannah knew restlessness only too well. She'd experienced it in her own career and observed it in those around her at some point or another. Sometimes people were just downright frustrated and couldn't put their finger on why. At other times it was because they wanted to push things forward and knew what it was that needed to be done, but were blocked by company procedures or other constraints that were out of their control. And then there were the people who really knew themselves, had purpose and a compelling vision and were restless in their passion for implementing it. People fascinated her ... their behaviour, development, interactions, the things that made them tick. So much so that it had motivated her to take up professional studies in leadership coaching and organizational behaviour.

Before creating her own business, Susannah was the Director of Organizational Effectiveness for McKnight Marshall, a well-known global consultancy. She had a natural gift for getting to the heart of what was happening for individuals, teams and in organizational culture. She was renowned in the consultancy field for this gift ... both within her company and with clients.

Susannah's passion for this subject (together with a conscious choice to travel abroad less for work and spend more time with her family) had motivated her to set up her own business. What's more, she was keen to select her own clients and was specific about who would be suitable. They had to be open to the process and commit to taking inspired actions, both within the sessions and during the time between. Inevitably it would be a tough journey at times and often emotional. After all, most people she worked with had a lifetime of patterns and habits that were usually inherited or learned behaviours they weren't even aware of. But it was important for them to go through the struggle to face their fears and challenge their patterns, instead of avoiding or being distracted away from them. And besides, it was from the struggles that the greatest learnings and personal growth came. The rewards of doing this work were immense.

THE VALUES PROCESS: DISCOVER, DEFINE, IGNITE

Susannah explained to William that during the values process, they would be following her formula of:

DISCOVER, DEFINE, IGNITE™

Session one would see William DISCOVERING his potential values. Susannah always started her coaching relationship with her clients by going through this process, because it sets the foundation for everything that would follow.

Following on from session one, William would be DEFINING what his values meant to him and also getting further clarity to check which ones truly resonated with him; and then in session two, he would go through a process with Susannah to DEFINE his priority order, which would really help everything become crystal clear about how he was showing up in the world and why. He would then be able to identify what needed to shift. Once these two sessions had taken place, William would then IGNITE his values, putting them into conscious action in all his decisions, communications, relationships and goals.

Values elicitation

Susannah started by finding out what William's existing experience of exploring values was; as he'd discovered when speaking to Steve, he had not been exposed to much more than his awareness of his own family values and the company values. She then set the scene and explained what they'd be doing. Then they dived straight into his first values coaching session.

Susannah worked in an intuitive way, actively listening to William; to what he was saying and, more importantly, not saying and she would ask him questions accordingly. She provoked his thought process with three powerful questions, specifically designed to help William elicit his values.

Powerful Question 1: What's important to you?

'What's important to you in your life?' William thought for a moment before responding: 'My family of course, my work, although that feels a bit weird right now, and doing the right thing. Is that what you mean?'

'Yes, that's great, whatever comes to mind. We'll go deeper in a little while. Carry on for now; let's just capture your words. What else is important?'

'My team, but I'm not sure I've shown that lately.'

Susannah noted he was being hard on himself, but she didn't interrupt his flow. It was vital that everything important to William came to the surface … they could work out whether or not these were his actual values later on.

This was the first time William had felt genuinely listened to – well, at work anyway – Rebecca did this naturally. But to be asked questions that made him stop, think and reflect was amazing, even though some were quite challenging.

'What else is important to you, William?'

'I love it when I get recognized or appreciated for doing things well. It's a bit of a raw subject though because this is what came up to bite me at the awards dinner.'

William had shared the story of his on-stage mess-up with Susannah at their initial 'get to know each other' meeting. Indeed, this was the catalyst for hiring her.

'It's okay, William, just because it "came up to bite you" doesn't mean it's not important,' she responded, repeating his words to connect him to how he felt about it. 'It's more likely to indicate that you weren't meeting it in a way that necessarily serves you. Again, let me capture it and we'll go deeper later. It's essential we keep the flow of what's coming to the surface just for now – so keep sharing and trust the process.'

Susannah went a little deeper on some of William's answers. 'And what does time with your family give you?' she asked, supporting him as they continued.

'Love, Security. Fun … well, when I get the chance! And it's also important that I can provide for them; I pride myself on that. Now you have asked me this question, it's really making me think. Love for my family is so very important to me. This is definitely one of those painful moments, you mentioned.'

Sensing how he was feeling, Susannah added, compassionately 'This is what happens William, when we really look at what's important, but what's great is that in recognizing this, you have the opportunity to make some changes.'

Susannah gave William some time to process this, before moving on to her next question …

'What does your work at Gant Foster give you?'

'It gives me security and a sense of belonging,' said William who was now in full flow. 'Well, I hope it does. When I consider how I've been feeling lately, maybe that's not the case. It used to be fun, exciting even, but not anymore.'

William held back on telling Susannah he was thinking about leaving his job. It was too much to focus on right now so he'd share his thoughts on that later.

'It gives me the ability to be successful. Hmmm ... looking back, your questionnaire really threw me on that one! The question "Define what success means to you?" Well, I used to think it gave me a sense of achievement, but I'm not so sure now. I like to be recognized for what I do, or rather I did until a couple of weeks ago before I started to question everything.' William was very uncomfortable about saying this after the awards evening, but shared it anyway because he knew it was better to get it all out in the open.

'What about your team?' Susannah continued, to keep momentum.

'I like the connection with other people and the sense of belonging, as if I'm part of something. I enjoy helping them develop by sharing my knowledge, in fact, I love helping people in general. Blast! This may be why I am feeling the way I do! I help everyone, because I think it's the right thing to do and I get a sense of satisfaction from it.'

Susannah decided to interject here and go a little deeper, as she sensed William was having a key awareness.

'How long does this sense of satisfaction last? Would you describe it as in the moment, an instant gratification?'

'Yes, that's exactly it,' exclaimed William, 'it lasts for a short while until something else happens and then I'm onto the next thing.'

'Okay, that's good clarity, the goal is for you to experience a long-term feeling of fulfilment – one that's more sustainable, which is what understanding and acting in alignment with your values will ultimately give you. I can see you're keen, William, so first things first – let's continue the values discovery part of the process, then define and ignite them, and before long you will be experiencing these feelings of fulfilment on a more regular basis, if of course you choose to, that is.'

William was surprised at some of his answers. He'd never been asked questions like this about himself before and he was being listened to in a completely new way. He also found he was starting to listen to himself as he opened up to Susannah.

'I'm questioning everything at the moment, even my own identity, who I really am. Do you think I'm having some kind of mid-life crisis?'

Susannah smiled compassionately. 'Let's look at this as a soul awakening … that's the way I prefer to put it and it's good you're questioning things as it helps the process. What else does your work give you?' she asked next, to keep his thoughts flowing. She was keen to get clarity on exactly what was going on with William. Once he'd got his core values discovered and defined, she could work with him to explore where he was and wasn't being true to himself, and then have a greater impact in helping him make the desired changes. Knowing his core values would give them a firm foundation to work from.

Talking to someone he didn't really know, but who was totally focused on him, was a brand new experience for William. Susannah was listening and playing back his words so he could gain clarity by hearing them again. This was a remarkable process, which he was finding surprisingly enlivening. He still wasn't sure where this was going, but he enjoyed being able to open up freely in a confidential environment.

'That's all I can think of at the moment regarding my work,' said William.

'Okay, so what else is important to you?'

'Freedom, feeling free is important … I used to be carefree in my university days and when I first started at Gant Foster. Now I feel trapped, like I'm not in control and on a treadmill. I wake up, get bombarded with emails, charge up on coffee, rush to the office … it's relentless. I don't feel like my life is my own. There are always demands from Eric, from my team and from the US office or the Asia Pacific offices … the different time zones mean our communications seem to be round the clock and it's hard to ignore or switch off. Then there are my children … they rightly deserve my attention yet they hardly see me. I feel like I have no choice, that I'm at the mercy of work pressures and demands on my time and I feel stuck.' William paused, and then let out a sigh of frustration.

Susannah allowed William to get everything out and reassured him it was okay. 'This is quite normal at this stage ... it's great you're being so open about everything. We're looking at your values, which are your foundations for everything you do, so it may seem a little uncomfortable at the moment, particularly as you are voicing what's rocking them, but that's normal too. We first need to elicit what they are and sometimes we have to break things down before you can rebuild from a solid foundation. You are on a journey of discovery to find out who William Cleverley is at his core ... his true self. Once you've discovered and defined your values and got the priority order for them, we'll see how they affect your choices. This will help you understand how you show up in your relationships, how you resolve conflicts and the impact on the goals you set and achieve. Your values really are at the heart of everything you do. They are your gut instinct or intuition made conscious.'

William continued 'Steve talked to me about nudges and listening to my intuition. I realized in the conversation that I've been ignoring quite a few nudges ... It's always a tough one isn't it? Knowing whether to follow or ignore them. I think I've just been shutting out the feelings of uneasiness and playing it safe.'

Susannah was really enjoying working with William. He seemed to be embracing the process and was very honest about himself, even if it was a little painful. He was already having some enlightening moments, which would help him to break through. The awarenesses alone meant he was already shifting and if he carried on like this she was convinced he'd be able to start

71

implementing some small steps straight away that would have an immediate impact on his life. This momentum would also stand him in good stead for when she got him to go deeper and face some of the things he'd previously been avoiding.

Powerful Question 2: What do you enjoy?

'What do you enjoy doing, William?'

William needed clarification. 'Do you mean at work?'

'Any aspect of your life … it could be a hobby, an activity you enjoy outside of work or something you haven't done for a while.'

William thought for a while and said: 'I used to enjoy cycling with my wife Rebecca and our children, Annabel and Tom, but we haven't done that for years. Actually, I think my bike's gone rusty in the shed!'

'And what does cycling give you?' Susannah corrected herself, 'Sorry, what *did* cycling give you?'

William laughed. 'Pure fun! Rebecca and I used to cycle while at university together and we thought it would be a great activity to share as a family. Actually it was. I'm not sure why we stopped?'

'I know this process can feel emotional, but, if you're happy to, please continue,' said Susannah reassuringly. 'Think of it like this – isn't it great you're realizing this now and not in 20 years' time? You have an opportunity to turn it around, well, if you choose to.'

'Of course I'm going to choose to, Susannah. I'm not sure how yet, but I will.'

'I believe you. In fact I know you will, just don't worry about the "how" right now.'

'I just have to trust the process, right?'

'Yes you do. Now let's continue, you're doing great! So tell me, what else does cycling give you?'

'It makes me feel free. Yes, being outdoors without a care in the world and with my family and nature.' That was a surprise to William. He really didn't expect to say it, but he was in full flow now and wanting to continue. 'It also makes me feel healthy and revitalized and… oh right, I think I can see where this is going. I'm really not being true to myself at all am I?

'I love adventure, fresh challenges and discovering new places. Rebecca and I were forever having adventures wherever we went together, before the kids were born. I wish we still could – just need to find the time!'

Susannah could sense the frustration William was feeling. 'It does seem that some things are not in alignment and that's okay at the moment because you're becoming AWARE and that's the first step to change. Let's keep going, just for a while, until we've explored all aspects of your life. We can capture what your potential values may be and see where you're in or out of alignment, and then what you can do about it.'

William remembered Susannah saying that the process shouldn't be rushed, and that he needed to trust it. There would also be work between sessions. But after haphazardly going through life not knowing his values for the last 47 years, the least he could do was give this his full attention for the next couple of weeks. He owed that to himself.

'What else do you enjoy?' asked Susannah.

'Learning … I love learning.'

'Can you expand a bit more on that? What is it specifically about learning that you love?'

'I love expanding my own knowledge and discovering new things really keeps me fresh and revitalized. I enjoy reading too, but I haven't really been doing much of that lately. Is this why I am feeling drained?'

'Yes possibly. Acting like someone you're not is exhausting, demotivating and hard work and yes it leads to being drained. Let's keep going and make sure we've elicited as many of your potential values as possible … then we'll get you to turn this around.'

'But I don't see how I can change this,' William replied impatiently. 'It's great knowing this stuff, but how am I going to find time to bring this into my already hectic life?'

'Remember, this is a process you must trust, not an overnight thing, but you will see some results pretty quickly, I assure you. You'll take steps each week and each month, that will bring about not just a change, but a transformation.'

Powerful Question 3: What frustrates you?

'So tell me, what frustrates you?'

William burst out laughing. 'That's easy – not achieving something straight away. You may have noticed I'm quite impatient,' he chuckled.

Susannah smiled. 'And what else?'

'People telling lies, having hidden agendas or not doing what they said they were going to do.'

'Okay, so what's the opposite of those things, which are really important to you? How would you prefer people to be around you?'

'To be honest and do things with integrity.'

William was getting the hang of this – finding the words that resonated for him, which could very well be his core values, though he had more work to do to define these before he would know for sure.

Additional intuitive questions

There were various other questions Susannah could ask – she followed her intuition:

'When was the last time you felt really alive and energized?'

'Helping Annabel and Tom with their homework. Exploring the countryside and having a day out with the family. I also enjoy time at our holiday home in Spain, even though I have ended up being ill a few times, and I look forward to our annual skiing holiday … it's one of the highlights each year for me.'

'What does helping Annabel and Tom with their homework give you?' Susannah could probably have guessed, but it wasn't for her to suggest, as it was part of the process for William to say it out loud and find the words that resonated for him.

'It's about sharing my knowledge, helping guide them and just being with them as we have a lot of fun, most of the time. It also gives me love and connection too, which are important.'

'What is it about skiing that you enjoy so much?'

'Reconnecting with the outdoors, the exhilaration of skiing, it's an adventure and just having so much fun as a family. It makes me feel secure and happy with them.'

Susannah picked up a few themes here that William had mentioned, which demonstrated his values appearing in all aspects of his life, not just his work. He was opening up and she was keen for him to continue. 'And work?' She enquired, encouraging him to carry on. 'When are you really alive and energized at work?'

'Helping my team progress and be the best they can. Actually, wait a minute. … I am hardly helping them if I'm getting things wrong myself!'

William's eyes opened wide with a sudden realization. … if he wasn't happy and being his true self, how could he expect others around him to be, especially at work or even with his family? He had high expectations of others but was living by a different standard himself. What impact was this behaviour and self-doubt having on those in his life? 'I feel like I have let myself and my family down. Especially Tom, my son, as I haven't been very supportive of his piano playing and even missed his concert. I know he was very disappointed and hurt by that and I realize now the impact that could have on him and what he loves doing.'

Susannah took the opportunity to work with William's raw emotion and intuitively asked, 'What did you do at school that you loved?'

'Err, art … I loved art!' he said, stunned by this latest recollection as he joined up the dots.

'What was it about art? What did it give you?' asked Susannah softly.

'I don't know really … the freedom to be creative and express myself.' He said, almost robotically. William was still grimacing at the thought of the effect he could be having on his team and his son Tom.

'How does this appear in your life now, William?'

'Err - it doesn't. Apparently I wasn't very good at it, according to my art teacher, so I dropped it.'

Susannah captured what he'd said about art at school. Plenty of her clients had passions for things from their childhood, which they'd then shut out. It only took one negative or unsupportive comment from a parent, friend or teacher and POW – a child's dream could be shattered, sending them on a journey of becoming someone they weren't. It's all too common to see people following society's 'norms' or someone else's 'norm' instead of being true to themselves.

Susannah could sense the cogs in William's mind were turning and decided not to push anymore on this subject. She'd planted a seed and it would be much more powerful if he came to his own conclusions. Besides, she could pick it up again with him in a future session. The focus now was on discovering his values.

'Would you like to take a moment, William?'

'No, it's okay. This really is powerful stuff isn't it?' He could already see why Steve had got huge benefit from it. The thought of Steve sparked another core value reminder. 'Health! I haven't said health and of course that's important to me, but I've been neglecting it. I totally get why I'm so restless now … I'm not honouring the things that are most important in my life. I love it when I'm full of energy and vitality, but it's been a while since I felt like that. Perhaps it's time to get the bike out this weekend!'

Susannah continued to work intuitively with William, asking more questions where relevant and playing back some of his answers for him to get deeper clarity. She challenged and supported him, exploring all aspects of his life – family, hobbies, work, free time – until she'd elicited a list of 'potential' values for William. They were in no particular order at this stage:

Love
Security
Fun
Recognition/Appreciation
Sense of Belonging
Providing
Achievement
Feeling Free
Helping Others/Sharing Knowledge
Adventure/Exploration

Connection
Learning
Integrity/Trust
Honesty/Fairness
Creativity/Expression
Health/Vitality

'When you look at these words, William, do they resonate? Are they your words?'

'Yup, they're me alright. Some are quite a surprise, but in a good way. They're things I'd forgotten about or buried away.'

'Well, you're aware now and that's what matters,' Susannah advocated. 'That's great. Some of these are likely to be your values and some may be descriptions you'll use to define your values, which we're coming on to next. And because you've been unaware of them consciously, it's likely you've not been acting in alignment with a lot of them … hence your restlessness.'

'Now that explains a lot,' said William.

'Also, did you notice the themes that came up in different areas of your life? For example, helping others was important at home and at work. Cycling made you "feel free", as did skiing and I'd intuit that's also important for you at work?'

'Yes, it is. I need to feel free to do things my way, but I'm not at the moment.'

'Don't worry, William, most people don't consciously know what their values are. When they discover them and then live them, it completely transforms everything. We'll come to that part soon enough, once you've done the defining work. And the focus in our next session is the priority order, which is very powerful indeed. You'll notice in the elicitation I allowed you to come up with the words because it's really important we don't let others put their interpretation on what is most important to you, and that includes me too.'

What does 'X' mean to you?

'Before we meet again I'd like you to have some reflective time and ask this question on each potential value in turn: What does "integrity" mean to me? What does "recognition" mean to me? And so on, until you've explored all the words on your list. You may find you amalgamate some of the potential values and that as you are reflecting, you discover that some of your values may be subsets of others. For example, and this is just hypothetical, let's say "freedom" means adventure and expression to you. These words will then become the definition rather than the core value. I hope that makes sense?'

'It does!' said William.

'Your list is quite long currently, and while there's no magic number for the amount of values you can have, you do need to be consciously living and leading in alignment with them on a daily basis. So take your time over this exercise and see where some of them may have similar themes and you can perhaps amalgamate them.'

William had some very interesting work to do before the next session with Susannah in two weeks' time. That's when he would prioritize his values to reveal and highlight why he did what he did. Why he experienced conflict, both internally and externally, and why he made certain decisions over others. And while William liked to achieve things quite quickly, he could at times be very reflective, especially with something as important as this. He certainly wanted to give it the time it deserved, he told Susannah.

Susannah laughed, 'Yes, please calm that impatient achiever streak! Where else in your life do you notice this pattern?'

'Everywhere! I always feel like I need to respond to emails as soon as they appear, answer every question my team asks and pick up the telephone the moment it rings.'

'And how does this serve you?' asked Susannah, encouraging William to explore this.

'Well, in one respect it serves me because I feel I've achieved, I can tick something off the list and I feel good in the moment. I'm seen to be efficient and doing really well. But I'm also so tired, exhausted and can't see things clearly if I rush headlong into them.'

Susannah could see what William was doing – he was keeping himself constantly busy and in 'doing mode', avoiding having any self- reflection time … until now that was … for previously he'd not been ready to 'go there'.

William was invited to take his list of 'potential values', DEFINE what each one meant to him and notice where they showed up in his life, either activated in a positive way or triggered in a negative way. He also had the option to decide if a word was right or if he wanted to replace it with one that resonated more.

Susannah then presented William with a blank journal. 'I'd like you to start recording your new realizations as you go through this process, note any definitions, any thoughts and any "aha" moments that you have. You will see how powerful this is as we go through the sessions.'

'And can I invite you to do something else,' said Susannah. 'Have you ever heard of the term "mindfulness"?'

'Is it one of those new meditation type things?'

'Similar,' said Susannah with a smile. 'But it's not really new – over the years human beings have simply slipped out of the habit of being "present" and have become task-based, reacting to everything as it happens. Technology, emails, social media, phones ringing – most of the population are becoming reactive rather than present and intentional. They've become human "doings" rather than human "beings". It's about being present in whatever situation you're in, giving it your full attention and noticing it. Would you like to try this?'

'Well, I'm not sure I'll be much good at it, but hey, I'll give it a go. I need to do something for sure … I can't carry on like this.'

'Good! It's a great daily habit for you to cultivate, but don't be hard on yourself … if you forget or drift into your old ways, remember the small steps – the key thing is you're aware. My invitation is to be present, be mindful as much as you can in all that you do. Notice if your thoughts distract, which they will, and just keep bringing them back to the present moment. When you're with your family give them your full focus, otherwise it's wasted time if you're thinking of other things. It will drain your energy instead of replenishing it. Be kind to yourself, William. If something doesn't work out or go as expected, take the learning and then let it go.'

William had already made several important new realizations and there was more work to do, but he could see some areas where he could make immediate changes, just from having the raised awareness. This was a powerful process indeed.

Your Discovery Questions

This exercise is for you, the reader

As you answer these, be aware that there are layers of answers. For example, your first answer could be 'family', to which you then need to ask the follow-on questions provided. Keep asking yourself the follow-on question until you get to an answer that resonates with you as a potential core value.

The Three Powerful Questions

Note – you may resonate with some of William's core values. If this is the case, please take the time to make your own definitions. As you define each of your values, you will get greater clarity and may find a different word that reflects your value better.

1. *What's **important** to you? What does that give you?*

2. *What do you **enjoy**? What does that give you?*

3. *What **frustrates** you?*

   • *Whatever the answer to this one is, ensure you turn it on its head and get the opposite that resonates with you. This is your value.*

Here is an additional question, which Susannah asked William. Take some time to reflect on this and see what values it elicits.

4. *What did you love as a child?*

   • *What can you draw from that, which will give you a clue to your values? (For example – if you loved art, that may have given you the value of Creativity.)*

85

The following question will help you gain real clarity on what your values mean to you. Take some time to do this with each of your values.

5. *Define – What does X mean to you?*

- *To get your definitions, insert each of your potential values in place of the X one by one*

6

Defining Your Values

ACTIVATING CORE VALUES

William was already noticing the impact of finding out what his core values could be. He'd made plans to go cycling with his family at the weekend and they were all excited about spending time together doing something they enjoyed. They were delighted to see his new-found lease of life. And as well as having some much-needed quality time with his family, there were health benefits too. William was enjoying this journey of discovery, and although at times some parts of the process were challenging, he could sense it was taking him to a better place. Steve was right.

Rebecca was wise enough to let the process unfold … she'd seen too many of her friends burn out, because they thought there was no other way. It made her happy to see William now taking a more conscious, proactive approach and she was very grateful to Steve for suggesting this option. Dare she believe she was getting her husband back? It was early days, but there were some positive signs. William was starting to implement his new way of being and Rebecca would support him and indeed allow the process to unfold. When he suggested the cycle ride, she'd responded enthusiastically. She knew William needed encouragement right now. And more than that, she found she'd really missed the bike rides they used to go on and thought it was a great idea.

William had work to do before his next session with Susannah – to notice which values were either positively activated or negatively triggered and the impact this had on him.

Being present and 'at choice'

William thoroughly enjoyed the cycle ride and in the main stayed present and mindful of how he was feeling, being connected to his family and his surroundings. He caught himself drifting a couple of times into thinking about the meeting the next day, but noticed and brought it back fairly quickly to the present moment with his family, cycling through the nature reserve, having fun, connecting, discovering and feeling free.

He noticed that when he drifted his energy drained, and when he was fully present with his family he felt energized and alive. Why on earth had he not noticed this before? Maybe it was because he wasn't aware. Or because he was firmly stuck in a rut and couldn't or wouldn't see a way out. Had he simply accepted it as the norm?

The mindfulness technique seemed a good way of helping William come back to the present moment and it was making a big difference to how his family were responding to him. He wondered if he had the courage to do more of it at work, though somehow it felt easier to practise at home. And maybe that was okay for now, keeping the high achiever at bay … he knew he still had much more to learn and heard Susannah's voice in his head reminding him to take small steps.

A sudden surge of guilt swept over William. For a moment he'd drifted off, but he remembered where he was and looked over to Tom.

'Come on, Son, I'll race you to the other side of the lake!'

Later that day he looked back on how much joy and fulfilment the day with his family had given him. Sure, he'd done things with his family at weekends before, but he was always preoccupied. This time was different … he'd felt present. And he also realized he hadn't looked at his phone the whole time!

William was beginning to understand the power of being 'at choice'. He'd really wanted to go on the cycle ride and chose to be fully present with his family. That was in complete contrast to the time he spent at the office where he mostly didn't feel he was 'at choice'. William had previously believed he had to do certain things in a certain way, but was now already wondering if he could choose to do things differently.

Being triggered

One of the instances that had triggered him recently was the weekly Senior Leadership Team meeting with his peers – Eric's other direct reports. He'd come out of the meeting feeling frustrated, drained and generally out of sorts. On reflection, he now realized that he hadn't said what he really wanted to because he hadn't felt free to express his views on the rebranding and repositioning that Gant Foster was engaged in. He'd thought it was because there wasn't enough time, but in reality that was just an excuse that covered over his lack of courage to speak up and express himself freely. There was no way he'd risk standing out or standing up for what he believed was right, for fear of ridicule, or worse, a sense of not belonging, especially in light of the event that had just happened. It also seemed a little bit competitive to get airtime, especially up against Paul, the Sales Director, who always seemed to have the lion's share of the meeting. Steve was the exception, but William knew his reasons for remaining quiet and respected them. William noticed there was a distinct lack of collaboration in the meeting. This bothered him but he knew he couldn't do anything about this just now and remembered – one step at a time!

Following the meeting, William had returned to his office to reflect, something he'd never have found time for before. The meeting had drained him so he knew this was a sign that some of his values had been triggered. He was frustrated with himself and the others, especially Paul, for taking over. And he was disappointed with Eric, who he thought hadn't controlled the meeting very well. But what was it specifically about the meeting, and what had it triggered for him? Well, it had definitely highlighted his value of feeling free because he hadn't felt free to say what he wanted. And while this may have been self-imposed, this value had definitely not been met. It had also impacted upon William's values of honesty and integrity … he hadn't been honest about how he really felt and he was certainly not doing the right thing. That's how he perceived it anyway. Aha! Here was a realization about the definition of his values! The word that resonated with him was honesty … it was so important he was honest and open, but he had been neither. He knew the approach Gant Foster was taking to the rebranding and repositioning was not quite right, yet he still hadn't spoken up. Why was that?

William continued to beat himself up and then justify it. He remembered, even if it felt a bit strange, that he was to practise being kinder to himself, so he switched his thinking. Maybe he was not ready to do this yet. Actually, if the truth was known, he was still fairly raw from the awards dinner and didn't feel secure enough to speak up. Although he felt uneasy about how the rebrand was being implemented, and knew something needed to change, he realized that perhaps he wasn't sure what the right way was. After all he was only just discovering his own core values. Maybe it was a blessing that he hadn't spoken up, as it would have only compounded what the others thought of him. His peers had been pleasant enough at the meeting, but he could sense some embarrassment in the air. Wow, this was a big difference … he'd gone from being the achiever wanting to do everything right away, to questioning whether it was the right time and reflecting. He still wasn't sure whether he was trying to justify it to make himself feel better, or if he was actually being kinder to himself. There was a fine line, but he was at choice, wasn't he? So he'd choose the kindness option.

William realized from his reflections that 'integrity' and 'doing the right thing' were all encompassed under honesty for him. Okay, at least he'd got clarity on one of his values from this experience and he could see why he felt drained. The meeting also impacted on 'feeling free' because he'd wanted to be free to express his thoughts yet he didn't. 'Security' was another ... he hadn't felt secure enough to speak, or a sense of 'belonging' because of the embarrassment hanging over him. Connection, recognition, helping others and achievement were also impacted upon and it most definitely wasn't fun! He had been well and truly triggered in more ways than one! He was doing some of the triggering himself by not honouring his own values, and some through how he'd allowed the behaviour of others to impact upon him.

During his reflection he asked himself if any of his values had been fulfilled. His value of connection was met through a brief chat with Steve, and just before the meeting started Melissa came over and asked how he was in a very genuine and sincere way. She didn't say too much, as it wasn't the right environment, but he knew she cared. No wonder he felt so on edge, demotivated and restless. It was all becoming clear, but what could he do about it? His impatience, together with an excitement that he was starting to see things differently, was coming through.

William decided to share this with Susannah at their next session and in the meantime captured it in his journal. The very nature of reflecting, staying present and then writing things down was uplifting. It helped him to 'let go' of the bad feelings much more easily ... progress was certainly being made!

Over the next couple of weeks William focused on going through each of his potential values, checking where they showed up in his life, where he felt energized and where he felt drained. He checked in to see if each word resonated with him and where there could be overlaps.

Adventure, exploring, new things and challenge all seemed to be activated at similar times, but the word that resonated most with him was adventure. He loved rising to a challenge at work, probably because it also had an impact on his achievement value, which he thought must be one of the highest.

Wow. How would it be to see work as an adventure? This was something he definitely wanted to try out – what if every challenge that came his way could be part of the adventure, some being more welcome than others? This new awareness and level of consciousness about how he viewed things was changing his life.

William was really looking forward to his next session with Susannah, where he would discover and define the priority order of his values and realize the impact this had on his decisions, relationships, behaviour, and, well … pretty much everything really. Susannah had said this was where the power lay. What he'd already discovered was extremely powerful and life-changing in itself, so he really couldn't wait for this next piece. Through the discovery of what was important to him, William had started to think differently and this, combined with the mindfulness to be more present, was starting to have a very positive effect on his wellbeing.

Your Discovery Questions

Take some time to review your own life, noticing where your values 'show up'.

1. *In what situations are you mindfully present?*

2. *Where do you feel you are 'at choice'/'not at choice'?*

3. *Where are your values being positively activated? (i.e you feel energized and alive).*

4. *Which of your values are being triggered? and in what situations? (i.e you feel demotivated, frustrated, angry).*

5. *What will you do differently as a result of your answers above?*

7

The Power of the Priority Order

'Hi, William,' said Susannah cheerfully, at the start of his next coaching session. 'You look much happier than when we first met. Tell me, what's been happening for you?'

'Well, this values stuff is amazing! I feel like it's something I should have always known and can't believe I've only just discovered it.'

'It's great you've discovered it now or even rediscovered some of it. It's about to bring some really positive changes in your life. And just to put you at ease, it's fairly normal to feel this way – most people don't truly know what their core values are, let alone the power of the priority order.'

William was eager. 'I can already guess. Achievement will definitely be high up there, because once I set my mind to something I don't rest until I've achieved it. That includes this process! Although I did mindfully take the time to reflect and journal too. I see the importance of this.'

'Let's see shall we? But just before we go through the process of the priority order, share with me what's happened since our last session, so we can double check to make sure these truly are your core values.'

William had sent Susannah a list of his values and what they meant to him in the days leading up to this coaching session, but she now wanted him to bring his words to life … and would challenge him if necessary to help him get deeper clarity.

'Adventure was a real surprise,' said William. 'But I didn't realize how much I love it. This is what it means for me: discovery, exploring, challenge. This shows up a lot when I'm on holiday in Spain, skiing or otherwise. I love exploring new places and discovering new things. At work I've never viewed it in this way, but I'm excited to look at work as an adventure. I love this way of "mix and matching" the themes into different parts of my life. Adventure is definitely one of my values.'

'Great distinction, William,' said Susannah, offering reassurance. 'And if it's this strong, it makes sense for it to show up in all areas.'

William continued. 'Honesty; this to me includes integrity, openness, doing what you say you will do and being respectful – fairness is encapsulated here, too, and expressing my truth.'

William paused. Now he was using Steve's words! 'Expressing my truth.' He still wasn't sure exactly what his own truth was, but he was getting much nearer to finding out. He'd never used the expression before in this way, or noticed its importance, until he'd reflected on what had happened since the meeting with the other members of the leadership team.

'When you asked what frustrated me and I said dishonesty and people not doing what they say they'll do, well, I experienced this yesterday in our Senior Leadership Team meeting. I didn't speak up and express myself how I really wanted to. Many of my values were triggered in that meeting and it helped to confirm that honesty is a very important value for me. I think that's why I felt so low afterwards. It was great having a realization and it made me calmer quicker than it would have previously, but what can I do about it, Susannah? It's one thing knowing I've been triggered, but I want to respond.'

'You will in good time, William. First of all we need to continue this process so you can use your values, their definition and the priority order much more consciously. Then I'll support you in how you put them into action. It's great you have this example which has helped you get clarity on so many of your values. It's also a perfect opportunity, once we have explored some more tools and techniques, to do things differently the next time…'

'Just as it's important for me to be honest and speak up, it's also important to me that people are honest and open in return and in that meeting there are always hidden agendas, which I really don't like. It was this that made me realize that fairness was also linked to honesty, for me.'

'It's good you have this clarity,' said Susannah. 'so how do you ensure you're always honest and open with others?'

97

William didn't expect that question.

'Oh, I do try to be.' He replied.

'Are you always honest with others?' Susannah questioned. 'And what about being honest and open with yourself, William?'

Damn! He'd never thought of it like that before and, come to think of it, Steve had also asked him this. He was aware he got agitated and triggered when others weren't honest and open with him, but never stopped to think whether he was being honest and open with himself. This process of discovering his values was actually revealing that he hadn't been open and honest with himself at all, so how could he expect others to be open and honest with him? This was another eye-opening moment for William. There's certainly more to this than simply establishing a list of values, he thought.

'This is good, William,' said Susannah. 'Another awareness. What's happening here is an inner conflict with your own value. We'll take a deeper look at it once you've placed your values in priority order. Are you starting to see how even when you know your values, you can still be out of alignment with them? They're a work in progress. After a while it will become second nature to check in when you feel restless and consciously course-correct as you go. Anyway, please continue..., what else did you discover?'

'Having connection is important to me. This includes spending time with my family and it also includes teamwork ... I've realized I'm becoming more conscious of this in the Senior Leadership Team meetings as it doesn't feel as though we are connected at all. It has had quite an impact on me. I know I can do better with my own team too. Also, being in nature gives me connection; this was surprising, as I hadn't thought about it in this way before. I really love being outdoors. It gives me time to connect and relate to myself and my thoughts.'

'Fun; laughter, camaraderie, humour, being playful with the kids. I've realized how important fun is to me and I'd virtually been having none. No wonder I felt so low.'

'This is great, William. Keep going,' said Susannah.

'Love; this is really important and my family are everything to me. It means support, kindness, compassion, honouring each other. This is really powerful talking about these things aloud. I've already started making some changes, but can see there's much more to it now.'

'It's good you're noticing and making the changes, and better to make the changes in your personal life first,' said Susannah. 'Let's see how they shape up once you have the values priority order and then we can explore some situations you've experienced and see how you can consciously ignite your values' so they really work well for you. Remember, "your values are your intuition made conscious", so the more you familiarize yourself with them, the more natural and intuitively you will act. And the really good news is you'll feel energized, because ultimately acting in line with your values is about being true to yourself. You're in control of your life, your decisions, the goals you set and how you communicate with others. So many people are at the mercy of others, or doing what they think they "should do" not what they want to, because they don't know who they truly are at their core. That's why they feel drained, demotivated and restless.'

'This is all great in principle and I can see it working in a lot of circumstances, but sometimes you just have to do what the company requires of you.'

'Of course, but you're always at choice as to how you do things and how you perceive them. There are times when you'll do things that may not meet all of your values, but you'll be at informed choice and know why you are putting your values "on hold" temporarily. This is so much more powerful than just going along with something because you think you should – and ultimately giving your personal power away as a result. One way gives you energy; the other drains your energy.'

'My personal power?' William was curious about that.

'Yes, your personal power. It resides within you. It's much easier to understand this once we're working with your values in their priority order.'

William continued explaining his values.

'Helping others is a big one for me. It means supporting others, caring and sharing my knowledge, though I'm questioning this a little at the moment. I'm not sure it's the best way! Contributing – to play my part in something bigger, not sure what, but I know there is something.'

'And how does this serve you?'

'I'm not sure I know what you mean,' said William. 'It makes me feel good.'

'For how long?'

'Oh, sometimes it's only momentarily, other times for longer. In the moment it takes my mind off other things ... I feel good when I'm giving to others. Surely that's okay?'

'Keep going,' said Susannah. 'Let's also explore where it has hindered you?'

'Nowhere I think,' replied William, who felt challenged and was unsure why Susannah was asking this question.

'A-ha. All our values have duality,' she said. 'They can serve you or hinder you, depending on how you operate within them. It's possible to conflict your own values.'

'I get it. If I'm honest and open, which are important values to me, then I can see where I've been hindered. I often say "yes" to others and help them before myself, which can put me behind with other things. Then I get frustrated and stressed. Because helping others is so important to me I usually put others first. How do I change this? This is a really tough one for me.'

'You can do this,' said Susannah reassuringly. 'You're already taking the first step, which is awareness. We'll use this as an example when we work with a tool called the "Triangle of Self-Leadership".'

'I'm having plenty of those light bulb "awareness" moments! This is so powerful and a little scary. Am I becoming someone different? Will others recognize the new me?'

'Well, I hope you become more of your true self … who you really are at your core. It seems like you've been acting like someone else for quite some time. The important thing is to make you aware and get this more balanced, so you're not doing it at your own expense and it is sustainable for you and others.'

Susannah had another question for William. 'Is sharing your knowledge always the best way to help other people? How would it be to empower them to use their own knowledge, then perhaps you'd be helping them even more?' she offered.

This was very exciting to William, even if some of it was a little deep. He could see a whole new way of being emerging and he wanted to crack this and get into action. He had work to do, and for once it was work he felt energized and enthusiastic about. He could already see the benefits of using this with his team.

William was keen to get to the next stage.

'Security; I had a big realization here. I think providing is part of security. It's really important for me to feel secure and provide security for my family too. This is what drives me to provide, so security encompasses this. I also like to have a sense of belonging within my family and any teams or groups that I'm part of. This also fits here and may overlap a little with connection, but I'm not sure at this stage. I think being in control fits here too, due to my desire for certainty.'

'That's perfectly okay, William, at least you know it's important. You can always amalgamate it with a different value later on. After all, they're your values and there will be times when you question them. You may even choose to move things around a little.'

William went on to the next value and what it meant to him.

'Feeling free; having choices is important and I felt like I had no choice until we started doing this work. Now that I realize that I can always be at choice, I already feel much freer. Being able to express myself freely, exploring, liberating, being at peace, all of these fit here. I've mentioned exploring under adventure, is that okay?'

'Yes, no problem. It's obviously important to you as it shows up in a couple of areas. Let me just check, do you think exploring is a value?'

William had thought about that. 'It's definitely a part of adventure and feeling free. I'm actually wondering if adventure and feeling free can be amalgamated, but then sometimes I can have one without the other so I'm not sure.'

'At this stage, William, if in doubt, leave it IN. You can make a decision once you have the order. Let's see how they resonate when you hear me play them back to you later.'

William continued. 'Recognition is definitely a value and means being recognized and appreciated for my skills and all I do with Gant Foster. Being recognized for helping my team and being noticed for how much I have achieved in my career. This was a tough one, Susannah, because of what happened at the awards evening. But I have been honest, this is how I was feeling about recognition – and think I still do. It's important to me, but from what I'm learning I think I may need to do some work around this.'

Susannah waited to be sure William had finished and said: 'Great insight and we can explore this further.'

'Once I have completed the priority order,' laughed William.

'Yes, you've got it! I think we've just got "health" and "learning" left for you to describe. What do they mean to you?'

'Health is all about vitality, having energy, feeling alive, motivated, fit and well and I don't think I have been honouring this one much at all, but I have started to now and it feels good. I prefer the word vitality though, as it resonates with me more. And I thought about learning for a while … I enjoy reading and discovering new things, which is why I love learning so much. I am also enjoying learning about myself; it really feels like an adventure, so I've put it under adventure … there's a nice link between the two.'

Susannah was now ready to help William with the priority order.

'I think I have a good idea of it,' said William. 'Achievement is bound to be near the top, along with security and recognition.'

'That's interesting,' said Susannah. 'Can I ask that you reserve judgement for now? Remember, this is not a logical process. If you try to do this through logic and put your values in order yourself, you're very likely to end up with the wrong order. We need to get to the default of who you truly are at your core and how you operate … that's why we're going to use an intuitive process that speaks directly to your unconscious mind and not your logical one. When dealing with what matters most to you in life, we'll look at this from a heart-centred point of view and invite your logical brain to step aside. Are you ready to go?'

William couldn't wait to get started. 'Yes, let's do it!'

Susannah proceeded to take William on a 20–30 minute journey using a visualization process to stress test and compare each of his values against each other, one by one.

'I want you to imagine you're going on a train journey and I am going to ask you to allow your intuition to guide you.'

'Oh, okay,' said William, 'why not!'

'Great! I'd like you to imagine that you have two suitcases, one in each hand. In one suitcase you have love and in the other you have recognition. You're about to board the train and the guard says, "I'm sorry sir, you can only bring one case on board." Which one would you take?'

'What!' said William. 'Only pick one?'

'Yes only one! Your intuitive thought is often the best way to do this.'

'Love,' said William. 'Then, it has to be love.'

'Okay great, let's keep going, William. I'll capture your answers. Love or security?'

William thought intently. It was tough. Did he really need to have security before he could really love?

'Security.'

'Love or fun?'

'Love.'

'Love or adventure?'

'Love is more important to me.'

And so Susannah continued, comparing each value to the other. The process wasn't as easy as he thought – being asked to choose one value over another was very difficult at times, which Susannah sensed.

'William, I know this is hard. You're making decisions on the things that matter most to you in life. But when we're through this process you'll be thankful because you'll have a great decision-making tool. Do you have to make tough decisions on a day-to-day basis?'

'Yes, of course.'

'Then keep going because once you have this priority order it will make your decision-making so much easier.'

William did find it difficult on several occasions, when Susannah stepped in with some additional questions.

'Feeling free or adventure?'

'Oooh, not sure.'

'Okay, can you feel free without adventure, William? Or do you have to have adventure to feel free?'

'Oh, that helps – yes I can feel free without it having to be an adventure and I have my best adventures when feeling free, so yes, feeling free is most important here.'

'Achievement or helping others?'

'Mmm – I have always thought of myself as an achiever, but helping others is more important here, I can't just achieve for the sake of it – helping others.'

'Adventure or vitality?'

'Well, I love adventure, but what's the point of having that without my vitality, so vitality it is.'

When William had completed his values stress testing comparison, Susannah added up the notches that she had been placing alongside each value during this intuitive process. She then ranked his values against each other and he was amazed at the order of priority that his values showed up as:

William's Priority Order
1. Honesty
2. Security
3. Vitality
4. Love
5. Feeling free
6. Adventure
7. Connection
8. Helping others
9. Fun
10. Recognition
11. Achievement

Susannah showed William his recently emerged priority list and how each value had scored. He was shocked. How on earth were recognition and achievement so low? How had he allowed himself to be driven by them so much? Susannah explained: 'They're on the list, so they are still important, William. But maybe you've been placing a higher importance on them at the expense of values that actually matter more?'

Is that why he didn't feel fulfilled and was so restless? Was it because he had been operating from his lowest values?

Susannah explained that this was an intuitive process[1] hence why it was best done this way. If William had just ordered his values himself, he would have used the logical side of his brain and ended

---

[1]For more details on this process and to see a video demonstration, go to www.TheRestlessExecutive.com/resources.

up with an order that purely represented how he thought he was operating right now and not who he truly was at his core. He now had a list based on his true priorities.

'What else do you notice about your list, William?'

'Well, the top ones do make sense because they're the most important. Adventure is the surprise ... I've never really thought about it in this way before and I can see now I haven't been honouring it.'

'It will be very interesting for you to look at life and your work as an adventure, William, I am sure.'

William was coming alive talking about the things that were important to him and that he enjoyed. It was obvious to him now – he felt alive because these things were his values. If he wasn't conscious of the very things that were driving his life, how many others weren't?

'What else stands out for you?' asked Susannah.

'Recognition. This has always been really important to me ... I get frustrated when others don't notice.'

'A-ha!' said Susannah. 'There are a couple of challenges with this one. Firstly, you've been allowing yourself to be driven by one of your values that are lower on the list to the detriment of some of the higher ones, which puts you out of alignment and makes you restless. Your soul knows and "nudges" you. And secondly, recognition is a value that could lend itself to being met by a reliance on others actions, therefore you are putting your happiness in someone else's hands.'

'Yes, I can see that now,' said William. This prompted him to ask: 'But, do our values change over time?'

'A very good question, William – what makes you ask?'

'Well, security is really important to me and I now understand how it plays a big part in most of my decisions, but I am not sure it always has been.'

'As different events and situations happen, William, the order of our values can change – perhaps this became higher since you had a family?'

'Yes that makes sense.'

The priority order was very powerful and Susannah suggested William take more time to explore what it meant to him. Susannah highlighted some areas below for William to reflect on:

- William had been driven by his value of helping others, yet it came eighth in his priority order, indicating that he would be much better activating the values above it first to be better placed to help others. By consciously igniting and honouring the higher values first, he would be more fulfilled. And by naturally meeting his higher ones first, he would be better able to help others, sometimes maybe even as a by-product. He also needed to address how he was helping himself, but more would come on this later.
- Vitality was a really important value for William, one of his top three, yet he hadn't been honouring it. This could be a

key contributing factor to his restlessness, as he was out of alignment and had an inner conflict with his own value.

- When Susannah had asked William what frustrated him during the elicitation, he had said people telling lies, having hidden agendas or not doing what they said they were going to do, which impacted his value of honesty. It was no surprise therefore that honesty was in the top three, as the things that really trigger people are likely to be impacting their top values.

- During the values stress test, William wasn't sure which was more important between adventure and feeling free and the results ultimately showed that they were next to each other with feeling free at five and adventure at six. On some occasions, he might consciously choose adventure over feeling free, but he would do so by making an informed decision to step into his value of adventure, maybe to solve a challenge.

Susannah went on to explain: 'There is a huge power in knowing why you are doing what you are doing and making more conscious and informed choices. If on some occasions your decision means you can't honour every value, at least you know why and can make peace with it, instead of feeling restless. It is also natural to be more motivated by your higher values, which means sometimes the lower ones need more motivation and a conscious choice to activate them.'

William had discovered and defined his values and their priority order. He now had a powerful decision-making tool and could be at conscious choice in all that he did. It would help him create healthy boundaries and know what to say 'yes' or indeed 'no' to.

Your Discovery Questions

At this point, you have hopefully discovered your values and defined what they mean to you. To complete your priority order, the best way to do this is either with someone else (ideally a coach) asking you the comparison questions.

Go to www.TheRestlessExecutive.com/resources and you will find a demonstration video of this process in action, together with a downloadable worksheet that will help you with the scoring and prioritizing.

You may want to record your answers in your journal.

1. *What surprised you and what will you do differently as a result of seeing your priority order?*

2. *Which values do you automatically default into and where do you need to consciously ignite into other values?*

3. *How are you honouring/not honouring your values?*

4. *Go through each value one by one and ask yourself on a scale of 1–10, how much am I living in line with this value? Based on your score, what one step can you take to improve this?*

8

Using Values with Conscious Intent

At the start of his next coaching session, Susannah explained that now William was aware of his values and the power of the priority order, it would be useful to look at where his values were impacting his life and how he could use them with more conscious intent.

TRIANGLE OF SELF-LEADERSHIP

'Okay, William, let's look at the importance of your personal leadership power.'

'My personal leadership power? I don't want power over others, isn't this what you and Steve would describe as ego-based?'

Susannah laughed. 'I love where your thought process is going, but no, this isn't about having power over others. It's about the power of knowing who you are, staying true to yourself and standing in this power, because that's where leadership starts. What I'm about to share will take courage to implement. You'll be changing the way you do things, by being your trueself and people will judge you for that … you may even find that some can't handle it.'

William looked a little shocked but stopped himself from interrupting and let Susannah continue.

'This is why most people are not being true to themselves. They worry what others think, they want to fit in and do what's "expected". We'll explore some concepts together, and then I'll support you through the process of implementing these in the world outside this room. I'm going to help you really remain at conscious choice and own your personal power in all that you do. Let's look at a model, which I call the 'Triangle of Self-Leadership'. Let's use your value of recognition as an example and what happened at the awards evening.'

'Do I have to relive that again?' asked William.

'Only if you choose to, but if we go there for this example, facing it again, with the approach I'm going to share with you, will help you release negative emotion around it. You'll even gain the gift of what that experience has taught you. Sometimes going into the pain is the best way of letting it go.'

'Okay, go on then … I have trusted the process so far,' said William apprehensively.

'At the awards dinner you were focusing on getting recognition for yourself. Is that correct?'

'Yes, but I'm not very proud of that now.'

'That's okay, stay with me. How could you guarantee you were going to get recognition that night?'

'I couldn't. I suppose I just hoped I would at the time.'

'So who was in control of you getting recognition and making you happy?'

'Eric? The people in the room?'

'Exactly! So how does it feel knowing you're putting your happiness in the hands of others?'

This question stumped William.

'I'll explain,' said Susannah. 'Recognition is one of your values, but you are expecting others to meet it for you to enable you to be happy, and that isn't sustainable. Remember how we've spoken about each and every one of us needing to take ownership and responsibility for everything that happens? Well, if you're dependent on someone else to fulfil your values, in this case people recognizing what you've done, you're never going to be fulfilled because you're not in control of what others do. This is quite normal, William. A lot of people aren't aware that they're expecting others to do things to meet their values. This is where a lot of the unconscious rules lie and where the triggers happen too, and we will get to explore both of those in a moment. The best way I can demonstrate how this plays out is with a diagram.'

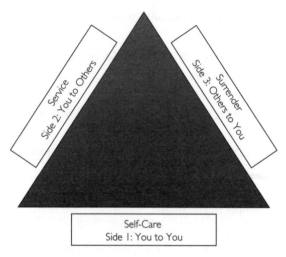

8.1 Triangle of Self-Leadership

'In this case we're using the example of recognition, but you can try this out on all your values one by one. Our personal power is within our control. It's our truth and who we are at our core. If we're not operating within a level of conscious awareness, we can give our power away to others. As an extreme, you may have heard the term "people pleasers"? In other words, doing things to make others happy, but often at your own expense. Saying "yes" to too many things, particularly things you don't actually want to do, is another drainer.'

'Yes, I get that only too well,' William confirmed.

'In order for us to feel truly fulfilled it's good if our values can be met in a healthy way, honouring all three sides of the triangle, yet we're only in control of two of them. Let's take your value of recognition, put it in the middle of the triangle and then look at each side in turn. The three sides of the triangle are Self-Care, Service and Surrender, in that order. Let me explain them to you now, and show you how they operate with your values.'

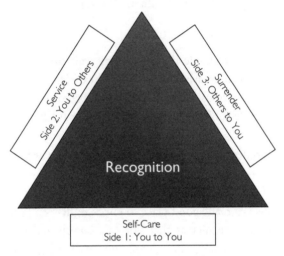

8.2 Triangle of Self-Leadership (with Recognition as the Value)

Side 1: Self-Care – You to You

'Self-leadership is being true to yourself, owning your personal power and leading from that place. It is being values driven and heart-centred and trusting yourself in each and every moment. This side of the triangle is the most important but is often overlooked at the expense of the other two. This is where true self-leadership begins – know how to operate here in conjunction with the other two sides and you will be delighted with the results.'

'So, William, how do you give your values to yourself? In this case, how often do you give yourself recognition for what you have done or achieved?'

'Erm, not very often,' said William. 'I haven't really thought of it like that.'

'That's fine, most people don't and they wait for others to meet their values for them, which in itself is an expectation that is often unmet and leads to us feel unfulfilled. We'll come on to this when we look at Side 3 of the triangle – Surrender (Others to You).'

'You're in control of being able to meet your values at Side 1, Self-Care (You to You). It falls along the base of the triangle as it provides the foundation for everything else, and if you are feeling restless, this is a really good place to check in first. In fact, it's vital all your values are met at this side by yourself and for yourself FIRST. Unfortunately, most people unconsciously go to Side 2, Service (You to Others) or Side 3, Surrender (Others to You) before putting the foundations in. However, neither of these will bring you long-term fulfilment if Side 1, Self-Care (You to You) isn't in place first. This is where leading yourself has to start. Leadership isn't just what you do within Gant Foster, we are all leaders in our own lives.'

'Wow,' William proclaimed. 'This is huge. This little triangle is very powerful, it's all very powerful in fact. Everyone should know this stuff!'

'Absolutely, they should, William, I couldn't agree with you more.'

Side 2: Service – You to Others

'Again, you're in control of this side of the triangle. But a little word of warning here … you need to ensure you're not giving the value to others at the expense of giving it to yourself first. This is another common area of imbalance. For example, people will freely help others and while this is admirable, it isn't if you're not meeting Side 1, Self-Care (You to You) first.'

William recognized this in himself. 'A-ha, this is what I have been doing, it makes sense now. I have been very good at helping others and I feel good about it in the moment, but then I can get annoyed because it's at the expense of something else. Now I see why you asked me to trust the process. It all seems to be building into a clearer picture. This, together with the priority order, makes me see how I have been operating and why I was feeling demotivated. I was giving Service (You to Others) without stepping into Self-Care (You to You) first?' he questioned.

'Yes, but in a way that wasn't really healthy, so it wasn't true service, William. Because when you haven't got Side 1, Self-Care (You to You) covered, you can't truly serve congruently,' Susannah replied.

'And this is not an uncommon occurrence, William. Operating at Service, (You to Others) is essential, but you must ensure you're meeting the value at Side 1, Self-Care (You to You) first. It will help when you look at your boundaries and decide which values you will and won't compromise on. You can then work out what you're prepared to say "yes" and "no" to. In fact, in your case,

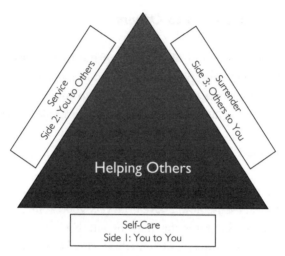

8.3 Triangle with Helping Others in the Centre

William, especially the no's, as I know that's more difficult for you. If we work this out in advance, it's easy to stand in our personal power and say "yes" or "no" more congruently. And as Side 2 is all about Service, this involves a combination of giving to others from your values and noticing what it is that is important to them at the same time.

'This is great, but how does it work with my other values?'

'Try them out – you can put them in the triangle one by one.'

'How about adventure?'

'You tell me, William – how do you think it will work?'

'Okay, so Side 1, Self-Care (You to You) – how would I give adventure to myself? Well, I see this discovery of my values and new awareness as an adventure, so that would fit there.'

'Side 2, Service (Me to Others) – I could create adventure at work, in some of the things I do with my team.'

'Great,' said Susannah, 'just one caveat – be aware of other people's values too, as you don't want to just impose your value of adventure. Find out what's important to others and likewise share what's important to you. It's very powerful for collaboration.'

'Oh yes, good point and I could see my interactions with others as an adventure too.'

'Brilliant – that works beautifully at Side 1, Service (You to Others) and let's come back to Side 3, Surrender (Others to You) once we have covered it in more detail. For you, with values of helping others, love and recognition, it is much healthier when you're meeting Side 1, Self-Care, first of all. Remember when you are on a plane, they tell you to put your own oxygen mask on before helping others.'

'Oh yes, of course, I see where it fits now, Steve mentioned this too. How could I help others without getting my own supply of oxygen? I need to do much more work at the You to You side, don't I?'

'Yes you do, and don't worry, you are not on your own here – most people need to focus more here!'

Side 3: Surrender – Others to You

'This side is the one we are usually aware of the least, but it triggers us the most. If you're operating at Side 3, Surrender, it's likely you've an expectation for others to meet your values and having an expectation is having a premeditated disappointment. If you are expecting someone else to meet your values, you're effectively putting your happiness in their hands. We need to take responsibility for our own values being met, by noticing which values we are expecting others to fulfill for us and then we need to work out how to fulfill those values for ourselves by going to Side 1 (Self-Care) first, then to Side 2 (Service) as we can take ownership and control on these two sides. We have no control on Side 3, so we therefore have to let go of it, hence the Surrendering part. Surrender the expectation and control of what you want the outcome to be – "let it go". Otherwise you will regularly be upset because of someone else's actions.'

William's jaw dropped, it was becoming more and more clear. How many times had he expected others to recognize him and respect him? Be honest with him? Trust him? He had a list! He saw now that he wasn't looking inwards at himself first and foremost ... he wasn't even sure if he was recognizing himself, let alone showing self-respect.

'And,' said Susannah, 'I notice you have a value of love. How's it going with Side 1? How are you giving love to yourself?'

William thought for a moment... He wasn't even sure he knew what that meant ... loving himself.

'Well, you've said that love includes kindness and compassion. This is why I suggested to you to start by being a little kinder and more compassionate to yourself, William? And perhaps stop beating yourself up about some of the things that have happened? Hey, these things have already happened, you can't change them, so why not laugh about them and see them as growth experiences? Our biggest mistakes are our greatest learnings, so with your love value and the kindness and compassion, you could use these to help yourself to move forwards.'

'I'll think about that,' said William. 'This is quite a new thing for me.'

'Of course, small steps, William. Remember, your achievement value came out lower than you thought, so how about stepping into some of your higher values more consciously?

'You said yourself that it would be good to see more things as an adventure and as this is a higher priority value for you, would it help if you were to see this experience as an adventure?'

'Yes, that's a great idea,' confirmed William.

Susannah continued 'Some values such as recognition, respect, appreciation, and acknowledgement lend themselves to be met at Side 3 first, if you aren't careful.

'What you'll find is that unless people become more aware of how to meet their values at Side 1: You to You and then Side 2: You to Others, they will be operating unknowingly at Side 3: Others to You, which is dangerous. Take an example of 'respect', as the value.

If someone is operating at Side 3, they're likely to insist others meet their values and in this case they'll insist on respect or hold an expectation that it's the responsibility of others to meet this value. In both cases, when this happens, they're putting their happiness in someone else's control and it will never be sustained. You are also likely to notice this more in others now, as well as yourself.'

'I can think of quite a few instances,' William said, thinking of Eric in particular.

'Whenever you notice this happening, William, you need to go straight to Side 1, Self-Care (You to You) and ask yourself, how can I give this value to myself and put the ownership and responsibility for meeting my values, back in my control, then notice the feeling of frustration dissipate?'

'That's ludicrous and amazing at the same time,' said William.

Susannah smiled. 'So, back to the triangle. If only one or two sides are being met, the remaining side(s) are, in effect, left open and you can give your personal power away quite easily. In an ideal situation, we want all three sides to be met.'

'But how will Side 3 ever be met if other people don't meet our values?' said William.

'That's where a little bit of magic can happen! Alternatively it's a great opportunity to stand in your personal power and strengthen your resilience. Focus on Side 1 (You to You) and Side 2 (You to Others), so you are activating Self-Care and Service in a healthy way and then watch what happens with Side 3 (Others to You). Take your value of honesty, for example. If you're operating at Side 1 and being honest with yourself (You to You) and at Side 2, being honest in your relationships with others (You to Others), and you Surrender or "let go" of the attachment and the need for others being honest to you (Side 3), one of two things will happen.'

William stepped in. 'I get the principle, but I can't go through life with people not being honest with me, it's my highest value.'

'We'll come to that. Remember, you're at conscious choice at all times and there are conversations you can have, absolutely, with people who aren't being honest to you. It doesn't mean you let them off the hook, but the aim is for us to be consciously working with our values and experiencing an inner peace and fulfilment on a more regular basis. I would love to say all the time, but we are works in progress and will have to consciously re-align as we go. For as long as you expect others to do something, you'll never have this. It will eat away at you and …'

William interrupted. 'And make me restless!'

'Yes!' Susannah laughed. 'It can make you restless. And when we "surrender" the expectation for others to meet our values and we feel a sense of inner peace, we approach the conversation that needs to be had from a centred place and can consciously communicate, rather than being irate or triggered.'

William liked the idea of this. 'An easier way to have difficult conversations with people.'

'You may not find them so difficult anymore,' said Susannah. 'I like to call them courageous conversations and I'll be encouraging you to put this into practice fairly soon, William.

'By putting your focus to Side 1, Self-Care, first, then Side 2 (Service) and letting go of the "need" for Side 3 to happen and just trusting that it will, that's where the magic happens. When we focus on what's in our control and let go of what's not and just trust, it comes back tenfold, and when it does, it's important that you receive it with gratitude. And on the flip side, if people aren't in line with our values and someone isn't, in this case, honest with you, then that's about them, not you. They're out of alignment somewhere or you don't have shared values and you have a decision to make. Are they that important to you? Do you really want them in your life? And if they have to be in your life, because perhaps you work with them, then it's about having a conversation with them – a courageous conversation from a centred place to share how you have been impacted and to understand what's important to them (their values); and who knows there may also be an opportunity to influence them and impart some of your wisdom! The conversation really does go so much better when you approach it this way. It has to because you are being true to yourself.'

'I can think of a few situations where this has happened recently,' said William.

'Perfect! You'll have some good opportunities to put this into practice right away then and do it differently.'

'Yes, I can't wait,' William said courageously, confidently and congruently. 'It feels easier already.'

'And just something else to note at Side 3, Surrender (Others to You), when you really do Surrender and let go of the attachment to what happens and it comes back to you, you need to be in "receive mode" and be thankful it came to you, without expectation. Just watch – this will happen when you very least expect it.

'In summary, focus on Self-care first, then Serve others in a way that is healthy and Surrender the expectation (which is ego-based) at Side 3 and enjoy the magic that happens.'

Being triggered

'Do you remember when we were eliciting your values, William, I asked what frustrated you?'

'Yes, absolutely,' replied William. 'I said people not doing what they say they'll do or being dishonest.'

'We're often triggered when a person, or an event, hasn't met one of our values,' said Susannah.

'A-ha, Side 3 of the triangle being affected,' said William.

'Yes, this is also where a lot of the triggers are activated and depending on how many of our values have been triggered, the worse we'll feel. We can also do this to ourselves, for example on the awards night. I hope you're starting to see the richness in what happened on that occasion, William?'

'Yes I am.' William cringed, and then changed his state. 'Oh, the wonderful awards night, the night that was an opportunity for me to receive many gifts of learning.'

'I love that, William.'

'Well, as we keep referring to it, I have decided to see it as an adventure and having some fun with it too also helps me to feel free.' He hadn't liked to keep thinking about it, but he could see there were so many learnings in it for him and changing the perspective on it had a liberating effect.

'So what values do you think you weren't meeting yourself that night, William?'

'Plenty of them; helping others, honesty, vitality, security, feeling free, love, adventure, respect … and that's just off the top of my head!'

'That's why you felt so awful and probably why it didn't work … you weren't meeting your own values or being true to yourself. It's time to let go of what happened, show yourself some love and compassion and forgive yourself (You to You); the reframe is a wonderful start. Be grateful for the experience, the learnings and how it got you to where you are now.'

William was okay with the reframe, he thought that forgiving himself may take a little longer, but he would try.

'You will get triggered again – just because you know your values, it doesn't mean this won't happen. But what it does mean is that it's easier to deal with and, in theory, you'll get to a calmer place more quickly. Then you can deal with it, either internally or by having a centred conversation with someone. And by understanding the other person a little more and what's important to them, as well as sharing what's important to you, you will find you get a richer, deeper relationship as a result.'

Inner conflict and the conflict loop

'So, is it possible that sometimes your own values can block you?' asked William.

'Yes, you can have an inner conflict on your values or you can get yourself into a conflict loop with them. The key here is knowing what to do with them ... the definition and priority order plays a big part in this. What made you ask that question, William? Do you have a specific situation or context that you are thinking of?'

'Yes, I have a couple ...'

1. Inner conflict

'I know we covered some things earlier when we looked at the priority order, but I would just like to get clarity on inner conflict. So, for example, when I wasn't honouring my value of vitality, I was out of alignment with it and as a consequence, restless.'

'Spot on,' Susannah confirmed.

'And also I could get inner conflict if I have a decision to make and I have to choose which values to honour, but can't pick all of them, like in the priority order exercise? And then if I am not operating effectively within the Triangle of Self-Leadership, this would cause an inner conflict for me?'

'All of these are great examples, William, and you now have the tools and techniques to identify them and deal with them more consciously.'

2. The conflict loop

'I would like to introduce you now to what happens when we have two values that are wanting to be met at the same time, but making a decision means we consciously have to step into one of them to break the conflict loop. This is easier with an example – do you have two values that you can potentially see causing you conflict, William?'

'Yes I do. It's the adventure and security thing. Sometimes I really want to take a risk and do something a little different, like shaking things up a little from the way we normally do things at Gant Foster, but then I stop myself because I'm not sure of the consequences and that makes me feel uncertain and insecure. A great start would be speaking up in the next Senior Leadership Team meeting. If I did this I know it would feel adventurous. I'd feel free and believe I'd be helping others. But I'm now seeing that my value of security, which is higher up the priority list, is stopping me and that's making me frustrated.'

'Great example – it does sound like you have a conflict loop within your own values and this happens to most of us at some point. In this case, you have adventure on one side of the loop, and security on the other. There will be situations where we meet some values and not others. We have to make a decision and it's tough, a bit like you experienced on the priority order exercise. When we have a values clash like this, it inevitably creates some inner turmoil and a little soul searching, as we know we want both things, and it's hard for us to know which one to go with. Ultimately, the more aware we are of our values, the more we can make conscious, informed choices and be at peace with them.'

'The easiest way to explain the way a conflict loop works and affects us is for me to draw a diagram.'

SECURITY

ADVENTURE

8.4 Conflict Loop Diagram

'In your example, for instance, you want to meet your value of security, and this being met allows you to feel secure, certain, etc. So, you put things in place to ensure your high value of security is being met, but after a while you may notice you are getting restless, because you are not doing as much to fulfil the other values, especially in this case, the value of adventure. That restless-ness makes you choose activities that will provide you with adventure; and then you become restless again, because you are not experiencing the security you want to. In a conflict loop, one of your core values will not be met whilst the other one is.

'You go around this loop until you can break out of it either through having the awareness alone that you are looping, or by you consciously choosing to step into one of the values and act on it, whilst knowing you may be moving away from a potentially higher priority value for a short period of time.

'Applying trust also helps; and you could end up with your security value ultimately being met at a deeper, more fulfilling level, if you honour some of your other values too.'

'Okay, let me just make sure I get that. So if I step into my adventure value, without so much emphasis on security and take the action related to adventure, I may actually feel more secure as a result, after taking a step out of my comfort zone. But I have to trust that by taking this leap of faith, it will work out?' asked William.

'Yes, and when you live and act in line with your values it will work. It may not be without challenge or discomfort, but ulti-mately it will work, it has to, because you're being true to yourself. What's happening with the loop is that you're meeting your value of security and then when you are feeling good with that, you edge towards your adventure value, so you do something to fulfil this value in that moment but avoid stepping into it fully to take the desired action. And then what will happen is that the other value (security) will then start pulling you back around the loop, and so on. At some point you need to choose to consciously step into your value of adventure and go for it, put that stake in the ground and trust yourself. And you're intuitive, William, we all are, so act on that and commit. Intuition is a huge part of being a courageous leader ... trusting yourself to do what you know is right deep down inside. Your values help you develop this because they put the intuitive thought or feeling into perspective. Also, because your security value is so important to you, you can choose to go there first and ask the following question: "What do I need to do, or what needs to happen, in order for me to feel the security I need, to let me step into the adventure that I want?"'

'Okay, so in order to feel more secure about taking the leap, I need to look at possible outcomes such as who I need to speak to or get on board in advance and weigh up the risks?,' asked William. 'That makes sense – I think I know why I've not been speaking up at the management meeting now. I've wanted to take the risk and say something about the rebranding and repositioning, which feels adventurous, but my security value has been stopping me. I won't know for sure until I do it. I can see that if I can find ways to feel more secure, I'll feel more able to freely say what I want to say, and I'll be more likely to do so. Also, I need to feel more secure in myself and trust myself to speak. If I'm being true to myself, what's the worst that can happen? I may get judged or others may disagree. But, if I carry on letting my own values block me I won't get anywhere!

'Susannah, I like this more and more, thank you for asking me that question. I hadn't thought of it like that. I still can't believe

I didn't know my values until now and most people are walking around half-asleep not knowing this stuff.' William smiled as he heard himself. He was getting really passionate and could now understand why Steve had waxed lyrical about it. He was beginning to feel a deeper sense of purpose emerging. Things were really shifting for him and all this in just over a month.

'Before you take the action, William, it's worth checking whether it aligns with your company values.'

'I will, but this the area I am wanting to challenge. I think we need to look at them in a deeper, more engaged way. I am seeing things very differently now.'

'So, are you beginning to see now how living in line with your values brings fulfilment? And while achievement is still important to you, it's more of a by-product of meeting your other values rather than a key driver. The way you were looking to constantly achieve, achieve, achieve, and the way many others do before they look for deeper meaning, isn't sustainable. It gives a momentary good feeling … instant gratification if you like. Being values driven as an individual, as a team and as a company is what gives you true fulfilment, inspiration, creativity, motivation, trust and ultimately sustainability and more profitable results. The results are, however, so much greater because they are not just about the numbers but about the richness and rewards of how they were achieved and it is that, which makes it truly fulfilling on every level.'

The rules that rule us

'William, there's one more area I'd like to cover today. The rules we all unconsciously attach to our values. We make conditions that have to be true for our values to be met. Let me offer an example – prior to these sessions you might have had a rule attached to your value of recognition that went something like this: People need to recognize all of my achievements. Here's another example. Let's say someone has a value of respect and they attach a rule that everyone needs to be on time for meetings as a mark of respect. Ultimately these rules will serve us to some degree, but also hinder us. A good way of spotting our rules is when we get triggered, which you now know how to do. Our rules generally show up at Side 3, well, the unhealthy ones anyway, and those are the ones we want to change. So, consider the "being on time for meetings" rule. Here we may find ourselves getting agitated when someone is late and we make ourselves stressed, so it's a good time to ask ourselves what has to be true for me to feel this way and see what pops out. Ultimately if it's not healthy, we need to change it.'

William laughed. 'I think you may have read my mind, Susannah, I hate people being late for meetings!'

'Ha ha, so it's a good one to use. Who gets upset, you or them?'

'Me,' said William.

'Okay, so you have a rule that doesn't serve you. What might a better rule be?'

'I'm not sure I follow this, Susannah.'

'Don't worry; this is the area that is more difficult to explain. I'll share this example and then we can work with another one of yours. A lot of unhealthy rules show up at Side 3 of the triangle because they often involve having expectations of others. A better rule instead of "people must always be on time for meetings" might be: "I'm always on time for meetings and I let go of controlling others"'.

'I see,' said William. 'That way the rule is mine and I haven't made it dependent on someone else doing something. But that doesn't make it right, does it?'

'No, and you can most definitely have a conversation to express your truth, but there's no point getting wound up over other people's actions. Get to the meeting on time and then have a centred conversation. But if you do it from this place, you'll be more at peace and have a better conversation. Out of interest, if this was one of your rules, which value would it be linked to?'

'Oh, that's easy, my honesty value, which for me encompasses fairness and respect and being late affects all of those – it would trigger me good and proper.'

'Now let's look at one of your examples, William ... I think I spotted one earlier. You shared how your value of helping others meant you sharing your knowledge?'

'Yes, that's right.'

'Are you happy to see if this is a rule that either helps or hinders you?'

'Of course, go for it!'

Susannah then went through the following sequence with William.

'Value: Helping others.

Rule: I share my knowledge with others to help them. How does that help you, William?'

'It makes me feel good about helping other people progress.'

'And how does it hinder you?'

'Well, from what I'm learning and from other people's reactions, they don't always want it. I think they'd be better owning the solutions themselves and I'm not letting them. I am imposing my values onto them, as we discussed earlier.'

'Okay, so let's keep the essence of what's good and what might be a better rule for you under the value of helping others.'

'New Rule: I listen to understand where people are at and ask quality questions before I offer to help them. Only then do I share my knowledge if it's appropriate. How does that feel?'[1]

---

[1] See More Resources.

'A lot lighter. I can still serve them, but in a way that actually helps them a lot more.'

'Excellent! And I also remember you saying that it's important to bring out the best in others too.'

'Oh yes, that would work really well. I may well change my new rule to include that, it makes it even healthier.'

'Of course, make it work for you, William, and see what else shows up for you over the coming weeks. And you've just hit on something there that would be useful for you to connect to.'

'I have?' said William, curiously.

'Yes, you said it felt a lot lighter. Noticing if something feels light or heavy is a great way to see if you're meeting your values and being true to yourself. It's the best way to tune in to your intuition. Let's close the session there for today … you've really taken on and embraced quite a lot. Look back and reflect on it, keep journalling and practise initially in situations where it feels safe. Then I want you to really start living your values and trusting your intuition in the way you live and lead on a daily basis.'

Your Discovery Questions

This chapter covered a variety of tools and techniques. Take some time to go through them with your own examples and record your realizations in your journal.

1. *Taking your values one by one, put them in the Triangle of Self-Leadership and examine where you are in relation to giving the value to yourself (Side 1, Self-Care), to others (Side 2, Service) or have an expectation of needing others to meet it for you (Side 3, Surrender).*

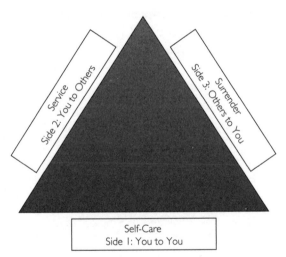

Self-Care
Side 1: You to You

8.5 Triangle of Self-Leadership

2. *Which of your values could be causing you inner conflict?*

3. *What can you do to resolve it?*

4. *Which of your values may be creating a conflict loop?*

5. *What rules do you have that serve you and you want to keep?*

6. *What rules do you have that don't serve you and you want to change? (It may be useful to look at situation that triggers you — this will help you to uncover unhealthy rules)*

(See www.TheRestlessExecutive.com/resources for a worksheet to help you re-write your rules and video demonstrations of the other tools contained in this chapter.)

PART 3

The Transformation

'When you live and act in line with your values, extraordinary things are possible, magic happens and the rewards are immense.'

9

Shared Values and Courageous Conversations

Williiam was now much more conscious of who he was. He increasingly understood the power of his values and it was time to ignite them even more. Ensuring his decisions and choices were aligned to his values and that he was building relationships through them, and confirming that the goals and intentions he set for the future were in line with them, made sense. It was also time for him to really trust and act on his intuition. If he planned his future, based on what was really important to him, he would actually enjoy the process and feel much happier and more fulfilled. The only person he needed to escape from was himself … his old self.

IGNITING VALUES

William had already begun his transformation and was no longer behaving as the person he was before discovering and defining his values. He was a different person now with new awareness, which he was acting on. A different version of William was emerging. In just a few weeks, the journey of understanding his values and the power of the priority order, the Triangle of Self-Leadership, the conflict loop and understanding his rules, had helped him change, yet the real proof was to come in the next part of the process … Igniting his values in all that he did.

He knew he had to let go of his old ways of being and show up as the new version of himself … the real version. It felt good that he knew he was going to do this, yet a little scary too. He wasn't sure exactly how it would all go, but he had a great foundation, some amazing insights and tools, and every ounce of his gut feeling, his intuition, his soul was saying 'William, you can do this, you absolutely CAN do this, and you must!'

William knew he'd have to consciously say no to some things and yes to others. He was going to have to be more honest, not just with himself, but with others too and it might be quite painful. People might judge him or react in indifferent ways, but he had to be prepared for that, because it couldn't be worse than how he had previously felt. Besides, Susannah had said: 'If you are honest and true to yourself and your values, it will work. It sometimes might not feel like it in the short term, because there could be fallout – others' reactions and upheavals to go through – but it will work out and you will feel a huge sense of relief and fulfilment in the process.'

There could be some casualties, William thought, but hey, he'd been the casualty all the way through this so he wasn't going to be talked out of it. Especially by people who felt threatened or didn't want him to change, because of where they were currently at. It would be better for them if he didn't change, so they could feel better about themselves. Seeing William step up was going to 'wobble' some people. He had decided to walk this path and stay true to himself, be a role model to others and set himself and others free from the worlds they created around themselves. The worlds that actually kept them trapped and playing small. Now that William had opened up to the possibility of exploring who he was, he realized that there was a bigger game to play and his sense of purpose was beginning to emerge.

William had already started to make changes, particularly at home. Rebecca had noticed how much happier he was in himself and this was reflected in his behaviour. He seemed calmer, less on edge and definitely more present.

They were cycling as a family most weekends and he was laughing and joking with the children much more. He'd even booked a restaurant for Rebecca and himself to have a proper date night – something he'd been putting off because usually something 'more important' came up. William had realized nothing was more important than spending time with his gorgeous wife … if he couldn't make at least one evening a week available for the two of them, then he wasn't honouring their relationship at all or his own values. The more William did to honour his values, the happier and more fulfilled he became and this had an impact on everyone around him. It was his turn to feel reborn and without having to go through a massive health scare.

Shared values

William had shared the impact of his coaching with Rebecca and also the values that had emerged as a result. She was extremely grateful William was going through this process and for the profound changes she was seeing in him.

And while William wasn't going to attempt to replicate how Susannah had coached him, he did ask Rebecca some of the same questions. 'What was important to her? What did she enjoy? What frustrated her?' It was a very enlightening conversation that revealed Rebecca found love, support and honesty very important, which William would have guessed. But what really surprised him was Rebecca saying how important it was for her to make a positive difference in the lives of those around her. Her family first and foremost, but she also held a deeper desire to do something else with her time. This was the first time Rebecca had voiced this and William was very supportive, offering to help with whatever she wanted to do.

They were learning more and more about each other and deepening their relationship at a whole new level. It was definitely a benefit that William had not foreseen but he was grateful for the chance to share his new 'self' and his discoveries with Rebecca.

William was keen to maintain the momentum and was about to step into that place of courage at work and start making more conscious choices and following his intuition. He was determined to express his truth, hold courageous conversations, resolve conflict with others, build values-based relationships and ensure his evolving goals, objectives and vision were all in alignment with his core values.

Opening up

Rebecca and Annabel were out late-night shopping to choose a dress for Annabel's prom, so William decided to seize the opportunity to have a man-to-man chat with Tom. He wasn't at all sure how it would go or indeed how it would be received, but he wanted to be open with Tom, which wasn't something that came easily to William. It was one thing putting this into practice where it was fairly safe, but quite another with his own son, where there were obvious emotional ties. William would usually carry on working in his home office, while Tom either studied or practised on the piano, so even approaching Tom for a chat was going to be a step away from the norm. But he remembered Susannah's words: 'If it's in line with your values, William, it will work, even if the result's not immediate.'

William took a deep breath. He knew he had to do this. Even if Tom only remembered this moment in ten years' time it would be worth it … he owed it to Tom and himself.

Tom was practising on the piano in the lounge when William approached him. He fell back into his armchair and sat and listened for a while, taking an interest in the talent his son was demonstrating. Tom looked over and stopped playing.

'Hi, Dad.'

'Hi, Tom, how's it going?'

'Oh, okay, you know … did you want to put the TV on?'

'No, I'm happy listening to you. What's that piece you're playing? It sounded great!'

'Nothing. Just a piece I'm practising,' said Tom, who was a bit startled by his father's sudden interest.

'Well, you played it beautifully. I'm proud of you for following your passion for the piano.'

'Okay, Dad, that's cool,' said Tom, closing the piano lid and thinking this was all a bit odd.

'Tom – I was enjoying that.'

'Uh oh, well, I don't feel like playing anymore.'

Tom had sensed over the years that his father wasn't that taken by his piano playing and this felt strange. Why was he suddenly taking an interest now? Tom was really enjoying their Sunday cycle rides together, though he'd never understood why his father worked so late and so hard. He adored him of course, but seeing him so tired was convincing him that he didn't want to follow in his footsteps.

'Shall we get some dinner together?' said William. 'There's a casserole in the oven.'

Tom thought that was a great idea, relishing the thought of spending some time alone with his Dad.

As they sat down to eat, William began by asking Tom how his day had been.

'Err, not so great. We had a double session of physics and I couldn't get to grips with some of the theories.'

In the past William would have jumped in to offer his knowledge, but he held back. This wasn't the topic of conversation he had in mind so he sympathized with his son to make him feel a little better.

'I'm sorry to hear that. I used to feel the same about algebra and all those confusing equations when I was at school.'

'Really? I thought you were really clever at school?'

Tom had always looked up to his father and didn't want to disappoint him. This was interesting to hear, that he'd felt the same. William was meeting Tom at the same level and really taking an interest.

'Oh, I don't know about that, Son.'

The last thing William wanted was recognition at this point. Of course, the old version of William would have loved this, but now all he wanted to do was have a chat about encouraging Tom to follow his own passion. So he went for it.

'Tom, can I share something with you that may surprise you?'

'Sure.' Tom was keen to hear, but found the conversation a little bit uncomfortable.

'When I was at school I really used to love art.'

'Oh, that's kind of cool.'

'Yes I suppose it was, but what I realize now is that I shut it off. I dropped art as a subject when we had to choose what to study for our exams. I didn't want to even think about it because I felt a failure.'

'Why, if you loved it so much?'

'Good question!'

William was beginning to think that Tom was ahead of the game here. Why on earth would anyone stop doing something they loved? Then again, that's exactly what he'd done all those years ago.

'Well, Tom, it's all too easy to listen to what other people say and in one of my school reports my teacher, Mr Robson, gave me a grade C and said my artwork wasn't as good as the previous year. I took this to mean I wasn't very good at art and decided not to carry on.'

'But, Dad, you enjoyed it! It was just a report for one year and it wasn't like you got an F. What do teachers know anyway?'

'I realize that now, but I've probably carried this feeling with me for years and I think that's why I chose a completely academic route. And I know a grade C isn't so bad, but I've always strived to achieve as much as I can, a little too much actually …'

William found he was flowing and Tom was not only listening, but being really caring about it all.

'Let me tell you something, Tom. Recently something happened at work that made me question everything – who I am, how I show up and why I have a need to achieve. I think it all goes back to when I was young and the art thing and my Dad, your Granddad, who was always working hard and keeping busy himself. He used to tell me hard work was important to succeed in life.'

'Are you having a mid-life crisis, Dad?' said Tom nervously, but with a smile on his face.

William laughed. 'Ha ha, I don't know, Tom, maybe I am. Anyway, what do you know about mid-life crises?'

William was shocked. Here he was asking his 13-year-old son his views on mid-life crisis. What on earth?!

'Oh, because Mike's dad had one last year,' replied Tom. 'And he had an affair with his secretary. You're not going to do that are you?'

'Of course not!' said William almost indignantly before realizing Tom could feel threatened. He softened his voice and continued.

'I'd never do that. I love your mum dearly and you and Annabel too. I'm just sorry I haven't been around as much as I'd like. I guess I got stuck in a certain way of operating and it became a habit. My "mid-life questioning" as I prefer to call it Tom, has made me realize what's really important so I'm making some changes and I just wanted you to know. It's important you know what happened to me because I'd hate for you to go the same route and stop your music.'

'Well, there's no chance of that, I love playing the piano.'

William thought he'd try some of the questions Susannah had asked him.

'What does playing the piano give you, Tom?'

'Huh….. ummm, well I enjoy it Dad. And I get lost in my own world, when I play.'

'Sounds great! Anything else?'

'I can say things through music that I just can't in words. Dad, are you psychoanalysing me?'

'No, not at all,' said William, wondering how his son knew that phrase. 'I'm just genuinely interested and wish I'd been asked these questions when I was your age.'

William went on to share with Tom what had happened at the awards evening. He felt quite vulnerable doing so and not as secure as he would like to feel, because he didn't know how Tom would react, but there was no hiding anymore and he seemed to be doing okay so far. He also talked about how he had discovered his values and what they meant to him and that this was why he had asked Tom the questions.

When William had finished, Tom gave him a hug, no words just a hug.

William fighting back the tears said: 'Thanks, Tom. And I just want you to know that whatever you decide to do, you have my full support and you must absolutely follow your passion. I want you to be you, don't allow anyone to put you down or tell you that you aren't good enough. You have huge potential and are growing into a fine young man.'

They were just finishing their conversation as they heard Rebecca and Annabel pull up on the drive. Tom responded: 'Yeah, I am kind of cool aren't I, Dad, and if you really want to hear me play the piano, then come to my concert next Tuesday evening. It starts at 7pm. I'd like that.'

'Sure thing,' said William, 'I would love to. I will be there.'

He knew that Tom was upset he had missed his concert previously and he was determined to put that right, he wouldn't get this time back. Tom smiled and hoped this time his Dad would come. He'd been upset last time, that his Dad hadn't made it, but recently he noticed that William was making a real effort to spend more time with him and he liked this.

* * *

As William drove to the office the next day he used the time to reflect on his conversation with Tom. Overall he was happy with how it went. He'd opened up and shown his vulnerable side and it seemed to work, though he was a bit shocked at the mid-life crisis question. But hey, at least that had given him a chance to reassure his son and mention how much he loved him, which was something he hadn't done for a while.

153

William didn't want to leave it there.

He was now starting to understand that what had happened at the awards ceremony was a huge opportunity, because it had led him on this amazing journey of self-discovery. He was listening more and understanding the significance of what Tom had said during their chat. He was concerned though – did his son really consider himself not to be clever just because he was struggling with physics? William didn't want him to go through life embedding that in the same way he'd done with his beliefs about art. He decided to leave it a few days and continue the conversation with Tom when the opportunity arose.

William made a mental note to have a chat with Annabel too. After all, he'd assumed everything was alright because she wanted to follow in his footsteps, but now he wondered what her drivers were for this, so he planned to open up a conversation with her too.

William hoped that the more opportunities he had to engage and listen to his children at a deeper level, the better their relationship would become. He'd managed to use Susannah's questions to gain a greater understanding about Tom. It also helped him get a deeper clarification about himself, as he shared his own stories and feelings. And what's more, it was fun finding out about his children and what they really loved. He now felt closer to them.

William didn't expect to feel so alive, energized and on top of the world after just a few weeks and knew this must be related to living in line with his values. The ones he'd ignited in his chat with Tom were honesty, security, helping others, feeling free to express, fun, love and connection ... and it was most definitely an adventure. The joy and motivation were returning to his life, and since he'd started cycling and eating more healthily, his vitality value was also being honoured. Why had he even joined a gym when it was clear he loved exercising outdoors and this met many more of his values? A confirmation from his check-up at the doctors showed that all he was doing was doing him good. His doctor told him not to overdo things, as he had previously had chest pains, but there was nothing showing as serious and it was likely to be the result of stress and anxiety. All the more reason for William to keep up his health and fitness and living his values.

He felt a real sense of achievement after his time with Tom and now realized why his value of achievement was lower down his list than he originally thought it would be. He'd just experienced a great example of how meeting all his higher values first meant it happened as a by-product. He hadn't even thought about recognition and had cringed when Tom had said 'I thought you were really clever at school Dad.' William was pleasantly surprised and reflected to himself, how truly powerful his new understanding and skills were. The conversation with Tom had sparked a momentum in William to put even more of his values in action and to start to tackle some things that were still not quite 'right' for him.

A COURAGEOUS CONVERSATION TO RESOLVE CONFLICT

William switched his focus to the day ahead. He'd decided to tackle the awkward situation he felt with Russell. He'd been afraid to face this in the past, mainly because he didn't know how. While it still felt uncomfortable, he knew he had to step into his courage and trust the process.

As William entered the office just before 8am he noticed Lynne was already at her desk working away. 'Morning, William,' she said cheerfully.

'Good morning, Lynne. How are you on this fine day?'

'I'm very well, thank you,' said Lynne, who was pleasantly surprised that William hadn't walked past her with his head down mumbling, which was usually the case.

William noticed her surprise and laughed. 'You haven't seen me like this for a while have you, Lynne? Get used to it because I've had some big realizations in the last few weeks and this is the new me. Actually it's the real me … the person I'd been hiding away.'

'Welcome back,' said Lynne. 'We've missed you.'

William was delighted he was being more open and enjoyed the responses just as much. He was on a roll; that was until he opened his laptop and spotted the email reminder for the client appreciation evening the following Tuesday at 7pm. His heart sank – it was the same evening as Tom's concert. What could he do? He couldn't let Tom down again, not after their chat, but Eric expected him to go. He was actually looking forward to the concert.

There was no time to consider his options right now because he'd asked Russell to meet him at 9am and wanted to think about his approach. Well, that and clear some of the international emails that were awaiting his response. That was another new rule he'd adopted … he no longer opened them over breakfast at home and he felt much calmer as a result.

Russell had been arguing with every suggestion and generally putting everyone else's ideas down. He was so cynical about the company rebrand and repositioning. And although deep down William shared some of those feelings, he wanted to understand more about why Russell was being so vocal and to see how he could resolve it for all concerned. William had been finding Russell really difficult to handle. All he wanted was to stop Russell being cynical and deliberately awkward. In team meetings he had no qualms, promising to take Russell's views on board before saying 'Let's hear from someone else' – which was the most he'd done so far. Now though, William had a new set of tools at his disposal.

Russell was always punctual so it was no surprise when he turned up at 8.59am … a trait William respected.

'Morning, Russell. Thanks for being on time.'

'Morning, William. No problem, it's important.'

'It certainly is,' said William, making a mental note to come back to this and ask why he thought it important. Maybe one of his values was driving this?

William decided to take the lead and get straight to the point. After all, Russell worked for him.

'I'd like us to have an open conversation about how I can help you communicate better, especially in team meetings.'

Russell was taken aback by this direct approach and responded immediately.

'Why? What is wrong with my communication style?'

William realized he hadn't opened the conversation very well and was perhaps a little complacent after his success with Tom. He was both nervous and excited to sort things out. He thought Russell would be accepting of his approach because of his own style, but obviously not. Was he even aware of it?

'Sorry, Russell, that came out a little blunt,' said William back-tracking. 'I didn't mean to imply there was anything wrong with it, it just doesn't always serve you and the team in the meetings.'

'Oh, okay,' said Russell, now feeling slightly frustrated. He knew he came over the loudest in meetings, but didn't know how to get people to listen to his point of view otherwise.

William decided to course-correct … 'Actually Russell, let's start again. It would be really good for me to understand a little more about what's important to you when you're sharing your views in meetings.'

William contemplated sharing his own journey and what discovering his values had done for him, but decided it was a little early for this, especially because he was still getting to grips with it and it was most important that he took the time to listen to Russell.

'I'd like people to listen to me, it's that simple. I don't feel they do. I'd also like to feel a little more respected because I have some valid views on why our strategy for aligning working practices isn't working well.' William knew Russell was probably right about that point. 'Let's face it, people aren't looking at the details and vital information is being missed' he said exasperated. 'There's a huge difference between how we operate here and how the other European offices are doing things. I'd love to get this sorted and make both our lives easier.'

William had never realized what the issue actually was, because Russell was so vocal and everyone usually switched off, himself included! His focus had always been on trying to create a calmer atmosphere rather than ask more questions, because he thought that would only encourage Russell. He'd also just experienced the benefit of the values question 'What's important to you?' in action. And in that moment something clicked for William – maybe Russell felt like he did, when he was in the Senior Leaders meeting? He just had a different way of showing it and was, of course, driven by different values to William. This was all starting to make sense now. It was one thing having his own personal awarenesses, but quite another to put it into practice with others. But, even if he didn't approach it quite right, he was beginning to see how the benefits of knowing and operating from his own values could have a really positive impact in all his communications and relationships. Life really could be different from now on, especially now he appreciated that other people had different values to his own, with different meanings and a different priority order.

Even though William hadn't thought about what Russell's values could be (and it was highly unlikely that Russell had either), the work he'd done himself allowed him to ask the right question and intuitively pick out what some of them could be.

William encouraged Russell to share more about his insights on working practices and sat back and listened, really listened. This, in turn, encouraged Russell to share more of his ideas ... he was calmer and clearly enjoying William's attention and interest.

William picked up that 'being listened to' and 'respect' were important to Russell, although he realized some of Russell's requirements in these areas involved having expectations at Side 3, Surrender (Others to You) of the Self-Leadership Triangle. William was giving Russell what he needed and what was relevant to move the situation forward. He realized he hadn't directly addressed Russell's communication style, which is what he originally called the meeting for, but what was happening now was powerful. This conversation and process was deepening their relationship and giving William a better understanding of what was driving Russell.

* * *

Russell left William's office feeling delighted that he'd actually been listened to.

William took some time out after their meeting, to reflect and journal what had just happened so he could share it with Susannah and work out what to do next. William understood how Russell had been operating at the 'Others to You' side of the triangle and perhaps that was why there had previously been conflict; yes, it was obvious now he was more aware of his own values, he too would likely have been operating at 'Others to You', wanting recognition and to feel secure in the way the meeting was going – hence why he wanted to move it on when conflict arose. So, here they were, each of them with a different set of values with different meanings and a different priority order, and while he didn't consciously know Russell's values, what he knew about his own, together with the questions to ask and consciously stepping into Service at the 'You to Others' side of the triangle, had allowed him to have a really powerful conversation.

William had just experienced a glimpse of how conflict could be resolved through understanding each other's values; he then wrote the following in his journal:

'What if we all knew and worked with each other's values in a more conscious way? We would then understand our similarities and differences and get the best out of each other. This could even mean we avoid conflict altogether and collaborate so much more effectively.'

Your Discovery Questions

So now it's your turn to understand more about your shared values and the courageous conversations you may need to have.

1. *What do you notice about your relationships which have shared values?*

2. *How can you use your new awareness of your own values to form a deeper connection with others?*

3. *Where do you need to resolve conflict with others and which values can you call upon to support you?*

4. *What courageous conversations do you need to have?*

5. *Which values do you need to ignite more consciously in your life/work?*

When will you take these actions?

10

Conscious Choices and Expressing Your Truth

A DECISION MADE

William now understood what Steve meant when he'd said 'You are always "at choice" conscious choice'. He always had a choice in any given moment, even if it didn't feel that way. He may not always be completely in line with all of his values, but he was aware of them and better able to make more informed choices.

Would it be different anywhere else? William realized that if he left Gant Foster he'd just be changing the external environment. Besides, he was getting a renewed excitement about what he was learning about himself and he remembered how much he used to love his work, particularly in the early years when he felt free to be himself. It was the internal that he'd needed to change, which he was making great progress on. If he left the company now, he'd simply be taking the same version of himself elsewhere. There must be so many people who run away from themselves, he thought, who take a new job because the grass seems greener. But it takes real courage to stay, look inside yourself and be the person you really are.

William was looking at his situation very differently now. It was an adventure, a challenge, a discovery; and when he saw it like that he came alive.

William decided to call Kate, the headhunter who'd previously approached him about a move away from Gant Foster. He intuitively knew that leaving was not the answer and now his values had made this conscious. In the past he'd been confused and clouded, but going through this process had helped him to gain a much deeper sense of clarity. Back then the obvious thing was to consider leaving, which was an exciting thought initially, but in reality it only served as a distraction. He now saw that he could use all his knowledge and experience of Gant Foster to apply changes from within that would be much more powerful because he had the longevity and understanding of how they operated – He had seen how change was accommodated in the past and now he had ideas for a new way of doing things.

'Hi, Kate, it's William Cleverley.'

'Hi, William. How are you?'

'I'm great. Fantastic actually, thank you for asking.'

'Wonderful, I can hear it in your voice. You sound very happy and full of energy.'

'Is it that noticeable?'

'Absolutely! You certainly sound more upbeat than during our previous conversations. What's changed, if you don't mind me asking?'

'Well, I have some great news that may not be so great for you.'

William decided there was no point prolonging this, and although the old version of him wouldn't want to let Kate down after she'd spent time arranging interviews, the new version had no hesitation igniting his values and expressing his truth.

'I've decided to stay at Gant Foster and bring about changes here. I feel very excited about it and now know leaving isn't the answer, even though the role you put me forward for is appealing. The energy and state of mind I was in while looking at this potential new role was the old me. In fact it wasn't even me at all ... I was being someone I wasn't and thought the answer was to leave. I was wrong.'

William recounted the journey he'd been on and explained about discovering his values and the impact this had had.

Kate was intrigued. 'William, that's amazing! Thank you so much for sharing this with me. It certainly sounds like a very powerful process. It's something I would certainly be interested in knowing more about personally and for us at SmartMatch. I think we have only paid it lip service in the past, but you sound like you genuinely know your values. I think we've been in danger of bypassing something that's essential, without knowing the true power of its impact. Imagine if we helped our candidates to know their values and the companies that engage us and hire our candidates … what if they understood this process too. You've given me something to think about and I'd love to pick up this conversation at another time, maybe over a lunch?'

'Yes, I'd be happy to do that, Kate. It's early days for me yet, but I can share what I've learned.'

'Great, let's do that. It's been a pleasure speaking to you and thanks again for sharing this with me … you've given me plenty of food for thought.'

William did not realize it, but in the days that followed, Kate started to review her company's values and, to a certain extent challenge them. Did they live them? What if all candidates went through the same process that William had described? Surely it would be a great asset in helping match people to roles more efficiently and effectively? A win for the candidate, a win for the client and a win for the company!

William came off the phone thinking he'd handled the situation very well and the conversation had gone better than expected. He hadn't apologized once for letting her down, whereas the old version of William most certainly would have. Anyway, there was no need to apologize because he was being true to himself. And as a result he'd formed a great relationship with Kate. His honesty had helped them both and he felt secure and free at the same time.

He remembered Susannah's words: 'Expressing your truth and living your values will bring rewards. People will respond positively when you behave as your true self, and if they don't, it's their issue.'

A CATCH-UP WITH STEVE

'Life changes when you almost lose it. You realize what's really important in the blink of an eye,' said Steve.

William understood this more now than before when he'd wondered whether someone else's wake-up call was really his own. He was thankful he hadn't had his own health scare and hoped his new lifestyle would prevent one in the future, but who really knew? Life has a funny way of stopping you if you don't listen. Maybe it would've just been a matter of time for William ... he hadn't made changes following his father's stroke, or when he'd missed Tom's concert or even following the awards night debacle. It was only after Steve had shared his own story that William had really taken any notice.

William was sitting in Steve's office. 'Now I feel good about myself. I don't want to eat poor food or go for a beer at lunchtime,' said William. 'I see now that it only gave me short-term gratification ... almost like I was using it as escapism ... It made me feel good in the moment and switched me off, but it was only ever temporary and when I got to my office I felt irritable. In the afternoon I'd be short with people and certainly didn't feel vital. My morning routine was a habit too. My trips to the coffee bar gave me instant comfort and connection, but not in a healthy or sustainable way. We'll have to go to that juice bar again, Steve, I enjoyed it there.'

'Steady on, you're interested in juice bars now? Be careful or you'll be meditating next!' Steve was joking, but delighted William had had this awareness.

'Meditating. Is that the same as mindfulness?'

'Similar. Both are designed to help you relax and switch off. I always start my day with 20 minutes' meditation where I focus on my breathing and let thoughts come and go. Sometimes I do a guided meditation listening to a CD; in fact, when I started I found it easier to listen to a guided meditation.'

'Next you'll be telling me you do yoga as well!'

'Funny you should say that because I do! Every Wednesday evening and Saturday morning. Do you want to join me?'

'Ha ha, I walked into that one, didn't I?!' said William. 'Thanks, but I'm not sure it's for me at the moment, but I've started cycling again and I'm practising some mindfulness techniques that help me be present more often. They both allow me to switch off and step into my value of vitality, which I wasn't aware I had until the coaching. I also went to see the doctor for a check-up and he gave me the all-clear. He said my chest pains were likely to be stress induced and for me to manage this better, which I am now addressing. I have you to thank for all of this, Steve.'

'This is wonderful to hear. I'm so pleased you've taken it on.'

'Thanks. And I'm eternally grateful to you for being there in my not so finest hour! And imparting your wisdom and supporting me on this journey of course.'

'It's my pleasure,' said Steve deciding this was a good moment to bring up the awards dinner.

'Are you going to talk to Jason?'

'Yes I am. I've been a bit of a coward and shut this out until now. But I feel in a good place since doing the values work so I'm ready to have an honest chat with him.'

'Great! And better to do it from your new energized self rather than from the old version of you.'

'You're right about that … it will be a much better conversation. I must admit, I'm a little nervous because I think I let him down during the awards ceremony.'

'You're bound to feel nervous. But compare that to how you'll feel if you don't address it. I'm sure it would drain your energy because you'd be forever thinking about it.'

'You're right. It's time for me to step into my courage.'

Expressing his truth with Jason

William headed back to his office and was about to send Jason an email when a voice inside him said: 'Pick up the phone and call him. Make it personal.' Could this be his intuition guiding him? The same intuition he'd shut out because he was so engrossed in his life and drained of energy that he couldn't hear it. And hey, it was a positive voice for a change!

William thought for a moment and picked up the phone. He was going to be courageous rather than hide behind an email.

Jason answered almost instantly, but William was prepared ... he was consciously igniting his values of honesty and feeling free to express his truth.

'Hi, Jason, it's William Cleverley.'

'Hey, William,' said Jason cheerfully.

'Jason, could we arrange a time to meet please ... maybe over a lunch one day this week or next? I owe you an apology. In fact I owe you more than an apology ... I'd also like to share something with you.'

'Sure, William, that would be great.'

Jason was keen to find out what William had to say, especially as he was so disappointed not to have received a bigger build-up to the announcement of the award he received. Besides, William held a position in the company that Jason coveted, so he saw the lunch as an opportunity to learn and progress.

'How's this Friday for you, Jason?' said William. 'Block out a couple of hours in your diary – I know a place down by the river.'

It was Friday lunchtime and while William waited for Jason in the reception area of Gant Foster, he noticed the company values statement on display for all to see and wondered how many people actually lived these values, made their decisions and developed better relationships in line with them. He saw them in a completely different light now he was aware of his own values.

Jason's arrival jolted William out of his pondering, though he made a mental note to come back to this line of thought later on. Who knows, with the progress he was making and his new-found confidence in this area, maybe he'd even have a chat with Eric about it! For now, he turned his attention fully to Jason.

Jason was a well-meaning and high-achieving guy. He worked for the highly results focused Sales Director, Paul Borello. Jason was ambitious and pushed hard, but hey, so did I at that age, thought William. Jason tended to be focused on himself, which meant he would often forget about other people as he strove for success.

William wanted to be fully present with Jason, so he saved the important conversation, until they sat down with their lunch.

'Jason, I'd like to start by offering you a full apology for not doing your award and your achievement justice.'

'Thank you, William, I appreciate that. I did realize you weren't yourself that night.'

'I'd not been myself for quite a long time, but I didn't realize it until recently.'

Jason wasn't quite sure how to behave or respond so he just listened.

'Jason, I realize this may not perhaps be the normal conversation you'd have in the workplace, but I want to share with you what happened before the awards evening and in the weeks following. I didn't realize it at the time, but that was a turning point for me, a real moment of awareness. And because, as a previous Rising Star, I was chosen to present the same award to you, I hope what I'm about to tell you will be of benefit.'

Jason was still feeling apprehensive, but could hear that this was important to William. He was being very transparent and courageous, qualities which Jason admired. He took another bite of salad and let William continue.

William took this as an opportunity to express his truth and hoped in the course of talking that what he shared would be of benefit to Jason. As he was speaking, he heard that little voice again, just nudging him along – if this conversation was useful to Jason, maybe he could also benefit others by sharing his story. As they ate, William made a mental note to come back to this line of thought.

William took a deep breath and began again.

'When I was asked to present your award I must admit I felt honoured that I was being recognized as a previous Rising Star to present to another Rising Star. It did wonders for my ego and at that particular time that's where I was … 100% focused on me. As I heard Melissa eloquently and unselfishly speaking during the previous award I suddenly thought "What on earth have I done? I've made this speech about me rather than Jason." I'd not taken the time to chat with you beforehand and wasn't thinking clearly. Let me be honest with you … I was feeling exhausted, stressed and under pressure from day-to-day demands. I'm not making excuses; that's just how it was. I'm not proud of that moment on stage, Jason, because I let you down, I didn't build you up or acknowledge what you had done; I didn't do you justice at all. What's more, you could say I made a fool of myself and, ironically, at the time I was so worried what others would think. I know now this was my ego and not my soul, it wasn't the real me.'

Jason thought he got it, though it was a bit deep! Ego and soul were not words that he was used to hearing, but he respected William so he nodded, smiled and encouraged him to continue.

'It's said that in your moments of failure you learn the most and, while none of us want to fail, if or when we do we must take the learnings or life will give us the message again only in a stronger, slightly more ugly way.' Now, even William wondered where that came from! 'Well, I learned plenty that evening, although I didn't think so at the time, and I have been learning to pay attention to the signs or "nudges", as I now call them. It led me to hire a coach and I've had many revelations since that night.'

After asking Jason's permission if he could share, William went on to speak about discovering his values and more about who he truly was. How he'd been behaving at home, his sole focus on achieving at all costs, and how he'd realized this wasn't fulfilling him at all.

'Jason, as well as an apology I'd like to give you the benefit of hindsight and offer my wisdom and support. I'm sharing what I've experienced because I know you are ambitious and I'd like to offer to provide guidance and mentoring so that you have someone to help you achieve what you want, maybe without going through as painful a time as I've had.'

Jason was clear about his career path. He was only 30 years old and wanted to achieve a director position within five years and, as far as he was concerned, he was well and truly on that path. He'd always respected William and he admired him now for opening up and sharing his experience. He knew that took courage and perhaps if he hadn't witnessed what happened with the awards, he may have just shrugged this off.

'Thank you for telling me this, William, I really appreciate it and will take it on board. It all sounds very interesting, but I'm not so sure about salad and juice though!'

William could see Jason was joking, but wanted to make a point anyway. 'Ah, maybe I should have checked with you first? I'm a bit overexcited to have rediscovered how important my health is and want others to feel the benefits too.'

'It's okay,' laughed Jason. 'I survived it and it was surprisingly tasty!'

As they went their separate ways Jason thought over what William had said. What if there really was something in it? Maybe he should ask William to mentor him. After all, William was in a role Jason would love to have, so he'd surely gain plenty from William's reflections, mistakes and new-found wisdom. And if he was going to be this honest, then he might be just the person who could help him progress. Yes, William would be a great mentor for him.

BEING TRUE TO HIMSELF

Things were going well for William. He was happy with his progress and was learning a lot. He did find that he had to course-correct a few times, but accepted this as part of the journey.

Now it was deep breath time as he knew he had to act on his intuition and be true to himself. The next Senior Leadership Team meeting was fast approaching and he knew he couldn't let another one go by without sharing his views on Gant Foster's rebranding and repositioning exercise. He also remembered how he'd left the last meeting feeling completely frustrated. Virtually none of his values had been met and, if he was honest, he'd felt slightly embarrassed given that it took place immediately after the awards evening. So now he had even more reason to fully ignite his values of honesty and adventure and maybe he would have some fun too!

He was making an informed decision to ignite his value of adventure, over his higher prioritized value of security, to avoid going around the conflict loop that often happened with these two values for him. And while previously he would have waivered due to his priority order and then waited until he felt more secure, now he knew he had to consciously choose to ignite his adventure value and just trust that the security would come later, as a result of him taking a leap of faith and expressing his truth.

William had thought about asking Eric for an extended slot. He usually gave an update on what was happening within operations but wanted more time to add in a few thoughts of his own. He decided not to ask for more time, because he'd have to explain his reasons to Eric and didn't want to be talked out of it. He knew it was too important and that he needed to say it.

William's slot was at the end of the meeting. When his turn came, he took a deep breath and spoke.

'I'd like to speak about something other than my usual update today. It's something that's affecting us all and will impact our business in the future and, in my view, not in a positive way.'

William was slightly nervous, but felt most of the team were listening so he continued.

'We all seem to be going along with the rebrand and repositioning without stopping to think what it really means and what we want it to do. Of course it's a good idea to revamp our image and engage our clients more, but we're doing it from the wrong place … with our egos. We're making it about Gant Foster and what we can do, rather than looking at it from how we can actually serve our clients better. What's more, we need to get our own staff engaged first rather than just roll out another set of values and behaviours that don't mean anything to them. Our people, our teams, will only connect to the organization's values when they know their own. It's about starting from the inside out, not the outside in, otherwise we're just spending more money and not doing it properly. Surely if we have all our teams engaged and buying in first, this will create better energy for the launch? And how did we create the new values anyway? I certainly didn't have a say in them.'

Eric was a little taken aback by William's strength and was actually quite impressed with how he owned the space confidently. This coaching must be working, he thought. However, he wasn't sure how to play this, as they were a fair way into the rebrand and repositioning and to stop it now would have an impact on so many areas … financially, time-wise and links to other projects that were planned off the back of it. Eric really didn't have the energy to change it all now and was certain the US offices wouldn't listen. Everyone was looking to Eric to respond first.

'Some interesting thoughts, William, thank you for sharing them. I'm sure the approach you described would be brilliant in an ideal world, but we are already in the midst of this project.' Eric was careful not to make a fool of William and wanted to acknowledge him, yet he also needed to head it off as there wasn't time on the agenda to go into this.

Across the table Steve was quietly thinking 'Go, William!' and was about to speak when William spoke again, very congruently and confidently and definitely owning his self-leadership power.

'I don't see how we can't look at this, Eric. Let's take a look at the new values, because as well as not being sure they are the right ones, I don't believe that as a company we are really aligned with these. Can we see ourselves truly living and breathing them in all that we do; in all our decisions, our communications and the objectives we set?' William then went through the new values one by one.

'Respect. Well, we're not fully respecting our staff for starters, nor our clients for that matter, as we are not inviting either of their views or communicating well enough to them.

'Doing the right thing at the right time. This speaks for itself ... we're not doing this in the right manner and the timing isn't right until we have all of our employees on board.

'Accelerating change for the good of everyone. We may be accelerating change, but is it for the good of everyone, and what exactly do we mean by everyone?

'Passionate about excellent service. Again, we can be passionate here, but if we are not all engaged, is excellent service and genuine passion really there? I question that too.

'Innovation through teamwork. The marketing team have come up with the values and I respect the process as I know they've put a lot of research and work into this. But what other teams have been involved?'

Steve came in quickly to support William and before anyone else spoke said: 'I think this is something that's worthy of exploring and giving more time to. We certainly want to get things right, don't we? And if we continue without honouring the new values then aren't we being hypocritical and out of alignment before we've even started? It will mean our values are just wallpaper, that we're merely stating them, but they're not really alive and active in the organization. They can't be unless we get full engagement and our people all know their own values too, otherwise they just don't connect and will pay them lip service as a result.'

Eric hadn't expected this at all and was thinking what to do. He had to admit there were some valid points ... the company hadn't thought of it in this way at all.

Melissa spoke next. 'I'm in two minds about this. You've raised some valid points, William, and have already made me think differently, but as Eric says we're so far down the line with this now I don't think we can go back.' Her team had been involved in this project along with the US team. 'We could look at ways to get the staff more on board though, rather than just running workshops introducing the values and expecting them to live them. We could rethink that I suppose.'

Melissa was an intelligent woman and William had a lot of time for her. She was very level-headed and often spoke as the voice of reason in these meetings. The fact she was prepared to take this on board and look at it differently was great, thought William. He'd spoken up, acted on his intuition and expressed his truth and was being listened to.

Paul, the Sales Director, spoke next. 'William, this is ridiculous! I don't believe we need to spend more time on this stuff. Let's just get it done and out into the world and then return our focus to getting results. We haven't got the time for all this waffle, and besides, it's not up to us anyway. We'll need to check with the US and they're already on to the next project and won't want to mess up timelines and deliverables. Besides, my team members have already started telling clients about the launch and our positioning, so let's not waste any more time on this.'

William was half expecting that response from Paul, who ran the sales team. If he were in his shoes with his targets he may well feel the same.

'I can see why you feel like that, Paul, as we all have different priorities, but I stand firm on this. We need to think about sustainability and if that means taking a hit on some things now, then so be it.'

William could hardly believe he was saying this, but he felt good … it was great sharing this freely.

Eric decided to call time on the meeting so he could have a chance to think about what to do. It was an interesting discussion and also a distracting one in his mind. He couldn't argue about it raising some thought-provoking issues and views, but it had also meant the meeting had now run over time and he didn't want to ruffle any more feathers.

Your Discovery Questions

Use this opportunity to trust your intuition and identify the areas where you need to either express your truth or be more true to you.

1. *What do you know you intuitively need to do and which values do you need to ignite to do it? (Something that you've perhaps been avoiding or putting off.)*

2. *What conscious choices do you now need to make?*

3. *In what situations do you need to express your truth (more)?*

4. *Where can you be more true to yourself?*

5. *What values-based decisions do you need to make?*

(These questions may call you to be more vulnerable – will you *go there?*)

11

Goals, Intentions and Visions

The timing for William's next coaching session with Susannah couldn't be better, arriving just a couple of days after he'd spoken up at the Senior Leadership Team meeting. He'd received quite a few comments and some interest afterwards, and even though Paul didn't agree with him he'd managed to have a reasonable conversation with him a few hours later and had found out what Paul was driven by.

William had more understanding now of what was behind the results-driven nature that he associated Paul with. He discovered Paul was also driven by excellence and success and wanted to keep momentum going, and while they didn't come to an amicable agreement, Paul felt as though he was being listened to. William had approached it in his new manner which had given him new insight and a calmer feeling afterwards than he would have previously experienced. Even Eric had left the meeting saying he'd think about it – whether he would or not was a different matter, but the main thing was William had consciously ignited his values, spoken from the heart, expressed his truth and no major disaster had happened. In fact, it had gone rather well.

Susannah was delighted to hear this and congratulated William. 'It's fantastic that you've really embraced this and, in this moment, what matters is that you expressed your truth and the experience you gained by doing this.'

'It was amazing! I experienced a sense of calm come over me and dare I say "a sense of peace" inside.'

'That's exactly how it feels when you're being true to yourself. And although I know you want the desired outcome of changes to the rebrand and repositioning, right now, but that's not what's significant here.'

Susannah let William share all he'd been doing with putting his values into action, asked questions to support his learning and challenged him in places.

'What went really well?' she asked.

'My conversations with Rebecca and Tom and the things I've changed in my personal life, as a result, are top of the list.'

'That's the best place to start,' said Susannah. 'It's amazing how putting your home life first actually has a huge impact on how you show up at work.'

William shared some other areas that had gone well and, in response to Susannah asking him what he found most challenging, he told her about his conversation with Russell and how he hadn't started well, but recovered it a little.

'That's okay, William, you did manage to course-correct and this will happen; not everything will go perfectly, especially the first time you reach out to someone new or try out one of the tools. The important thing is to stay open, as you did, and go with your intuition and have the conversation consciously. Remember, your achievement value is now lower on your priority order than you originally thought it would be – what difference has that made?'

This made William think. 'Well, it's still early days but I'm not striving so much to tick things off, get them perfect or be in "I must achieve at the expense of everything else" mode and I think I'm actually achieving more as a result. I am also aware that I ignite my connection value more regularly.'

'This is truly great to hear and you will always get another opportunity – for example, with Russell and the Senior Leadership Team and you can build on your learnings.'

BEING TESTED AND MAKING A VALUES-BASED DECISION

'Speaking of other opportunities,' said William, 'something happened that's created a real dilemma for me. It's Tom – I've built some bridges with him and feel more connected than I have been for a long time. After I started to understand his love of music I felt so bad for missing his last piano concert so I promised to go to his next one on Tuesday evening. I genuinely want to go and show my support.'

'So, what's the dilemma, William?'

'It's on the same evening as Gant Foster's client appreciation evening and I'm expected to go,' said William with frustration in his voice.

'What other options are available, William?'

'I don't think there are any. I can't let Eric down again, so I have to be there and show I can hold my own in front of people.'

'For what purpose, William? Where's this coming from, your ego or your soul?'

'Well, it's my responsibility and is expected. Normally I wouldn't hesitate because I enjoy connecting with our clients in a more informal setting. Err, it's my ego isn't it? I'm worrying what others might think and putting an expectation on it, aren't I? It's "Others to You" on the Triangle of Self-Leadership?'

'Sounds like that to me,' agreed Susannah. 'And it's best not to make decisions from your ego. Let's check, which of your values would it meet?'

'Well, connection I suppose and helping others mainly. I probably wouldn't feel very secure and definitely not free, as I'll constantly be thinking about Tom's concert, how on earth am I going to tell him? It's an appreciation evening. I would be recognizing others, rather than striving for it myself, and that would be good for me.'

'This is a great situation for you to make a values-based decision, William. Let's explore which values would be met if you went to Tom's concert.'

'Oh, that's easy, nearly all of them! Honesty, I'd feel secure and connected, which is actually linked to my love value, so this would be in place more than at the client evening. I'd feel free. It's a new adventure for me to share with Tom and it would be fun too.'

'So you now have a choice. I think it's obvious which one is more in line with your values simply by listening to your energy when you spoke about them both.'

William agreed. 'I'm much more excited about Tom's concert, especially after our chat together, but it's not as easy as that.'

'Whichever decision you make, it's important to be at peace with it. Sometimes we have to make decisions that aren't in line with our values, but at least if we know why, we can make an informed decision.'

'Okay I get it, because sometimes, especially at work, I may need to make choices that are out of alignment due to other constraints. I must admit I'd been thinking whether it was possible to live in line with my values all of the time. But how am I going to explain this to Tom?'

'So have you made your decision, William? Are you saying yes to the client appreciation evening and no to Tom?'

'I don't see I have much choice!' said William, reluctantly. Then he laughed, 'Oh, I always have a choice, don't I?'

'Yes you do, William! Of course there may be consequences to both, so let me ask again, what other options do you have?'

'I guess I could ask someone else to go on my behalf, but I'd have to clear it with Eric first and that could be tricky.'

'But what's most important to you, William?'

'Going to Tom's concert of course. I have to go, I just need to make the decision and then be honest with Eric. I know what I'll do ... I will ask Russell if he'd go on my behalf! I wouldn't have chosen him in the past, but I need to show him some trust and he'd probably jump at the chance. If I brief him, he'll easily be able to do it, especially given his desire to collect details and get all the facts. It could really benefit our relationship and is a great solution ... one I have no issue telling Eric about.'

'This is also a good opportunity to check in with your rules,' said Susannah.

'Oh yes,' replied William, 'good one, maybe this had something to do with my honesty value, which incorporates me "doing the right thing". Do you know I think I have an unhealthy rule that I have been running, which is something like "I always need to be involved to ensure the right thing is done" but this isn't helping anyone. Wow, I can see where this shows up in other areas too, I need to change this straight away!'

'What would be a more healthy, empowering rule for you, William?'

'"I trust others to do the right thing", there, it's that simple and I need to "surrender" at the Others to You side of the triangle, letting go of control and expectation and just trust. I actually feel so much freer and lighter as a result of this shift. Thank you!'

'You did all the work,' said Susannah. 'I just asked the right questions. Be aware that the more you're true to yourself and begin to master this, that life has a habit of testing you, just as in this instance.'

'Yes, but they were the questions I needed to hear and wouldn't think to ask myself. And it's very interesting about being tested … I think I passed that one, so bring it on!'

ALIGNING VISION, GOALS AND BELIEFS

Now William was getting into his stride with his decisions, conversations and in his relationships, Susannah thought it a good time to encourage wider thinking to ensure the goals and objectives William was setting for himself were in line with his values and beliefs and that these were all encompassed by his overall vision.

Susannah shared the following model with William and explained that he now had his values as his foundations and it's important that they're first of all aligned with his beliefs (his mindset). 'It's all very well being in line with your values, but if you don't believe something is possible it's unlikely you'll achieve it. Conversely, you may believe it's possible without feeling driven or motivated enough to want to do it at the values level. Both of these create dis-alignment.'

Susannah didn't want to overload William at this stage by going too deep into his vision and goals, as he already had plenty to take in. He'd be doing a full visioning session with her in a few weeks, but it was good to get some initial ideas out and allow him to think about it.

William shared that he'd already set some personal and professional goals across his values. He knew not every goal needed to represent all of his values and he had created a balance across all of them. He was happy that his goals were aligned and he felt engaged and motivated by them.

11.1 Vision and Values Alignment

Personal

- I spend weekends with my family
- I have a date night once a week with Rebecca
- I cycle, swim or walk five out of seven days

Professional

- I help my team to discover their values
- I influence change in Gant Foster, specifically in the area of trust and culture
- I am contributing to something bigger than me

After William had shared his goals, Susannah helped him to shape them into positive and present tense statements and would explain the importance of this later on.

'I'm also aware that some of the objectives I have at work aren't completely in line with my values,' said William.

'Can you give me an example?' replied Susannah.

'Of course. I have to write a full report and business case each month based on our actual and forward projections, including why we're doing certain things in a certain way. It's really time-consuming and draining.'

'This is likely to happen in most organizations, William. There will always be things that you don't find inspiring or motivating, so it's good to look at how you could approach it differently by asking yourself which of your values you CAN draw on to help you.'

'I'm not sure I get that,' said William. 'Can you give me an example?'

'Sure. I'd guess you're honouring your value of honesty when you complete the report?'

'Yes,' said William. 'But not much more. It's not really much fun, my vitality value isn't activated, I definitely don't feel free and it can't really be classed as an adventure.'

'So how could you link those values to it, William? How could you feel freer, for example, while writing the report?'

'I suppose I could write it earlier rather than at the last minute, then I'd feel more free.'

'And vitality, William, how would you be able to lean into this one and gain energy to write the report?'

'Errmm … not do it alone I suppose,' said William. 'I could get Ben to help me brainstorm and mind map it out first … that would engage my connection and teamwork as well. And I could see that I'd be more secure knowing it's done before the deadline. But, Susannah, please don't ask me to make this an adventure, because I'm most definitely not adding that one.'

Susannah laughed. 'No, I won't do that. It doesn't have to meet them all, you just need to find a way to engage some of them so you achieve it more easily and enjoy it a little too.'

'That sounds good, I like that. Thinking differently to engage my values in all I do. Great, another tool for my kitbag.'

William then went on to share that he knew there were more goals he could set, but he was worried some weren't very specific. 'I've always been taught to write specific, measurable and time-bound goals, but it feels like I'm trying to force some of them,' said William.

'William, you're taking huge strides so don't put pressure on yourself. As you say, it's important not to force them, but let them evolve naturally and there are some pretty big ideas you have in there, especially about influencing change in Gant Foster and contributing to something bigger than yourself.'

'Yes,' said William. 'I'm not exactly sure what it is, but I'm feeling so thankful for the discoveries I'm making. I'd like to give back somehow, to make more of a contribution and for my life to have more meaning. Does that make sense?'

'Absolutely,' replied Susannah. 'It's great it's emerging; we can dig a little deeper when we do the vision work. We'll set a day aside for that away from the office to give you more space to think, to gain perspective and allow you to get creative with ideas.'

'Sounds good and I'm particularly keen to make a bigger impact within Gant Foster. I feel like, with all I know about the company and my new skills and deeper understanding, I can make a bigger contribution. I'm not sure I valued just what longevity can add to a company in combination with being motivated and committed. I now know I have to act on what I believe in and on what I know needs to change.'

As this was flowing out Susannah decided to capture it and ask a couple more questions.

'When you say helping others, who do you mean, William? Is it everyone or a specific group of people?'

'Well, I just want people to see they're all leaders and don't need fancy titles. We're all leaders in our own lives, personally and professionally.'

'Great, so it could be about people recognizing their inner leader?' Susannah suggested.

'Oh, I like that,' said William. 'Makes sense and there's something about building a culture of trust. I can see how understanding values and listening to your intuition can really help to develop and build this within people.'

'It feels like your purpose is emerging, William.'

'Yes it does doesn't it!' said William, feeling very pleased with himself. 'I don't feel like I have it fully defined yet. Do I need a purpose or a mission statement?'

'Yes, if you wish and you think it will support you. It will come, William; you've sown the seeds and the essence is there.'

'Let me say something out loud and see how it sounds,' said William. '"To help people recognize their inner leader, be authentic and build a culture of trust." It's not quite there, but I'm happy with this for now.'

'Good,' said Susannah. 'Everything doesn't have to be set in stone right away. You can have an idea and allow it to percolate and let your intuition guide you. A great way of doing this is to set intentions rather than goals.'

'Interesting,' said William, keen to learn more about developing his intuition. 'Please give me an example.'

'Sure. You'd set an intention in the present tense and make sure it's positive and then use it as a stake in the ground to activate your intuition. Here are a few different examples:

"I allow myself to live more consciously and be present in each moment."
"I attract the right people to support me with my purpose and who share my vision."
"I lead from the heart with kindness and compassion."

'This then allows more than one fixed outcome. Sometimes when we set goals, we get so fixed on how we're going to achieve them and quite often there's a better way yet we don't see it. Whereas with an intention, it opens up for your intuition to guide you and allows you to be open to opportunities that may show up. And because you've set the intention, your unconscious mind will go to work to find situations that match and bring them to your awareness.'

'I like this,' said William. 'I like it a lot! So, in the second one, for example, "I attract the right people to support me with my purpose and who share my vision." I'm not saying which people specifically, but because I have set an intention, I'm more likely to notice who is aligned and supportive?'

'Exactly!' said Susannah. 'And it can also be done the other way round. You may get an intuitive hunch, a nudge, and you can ground it with an intention, which in turn sets your intuition to work, which then generates inspired actions for you to act on. So, you might get an intuition that a certain person could be good to work alongside and it makes you think about creating a group of people, but you're not sure who the others will be. So, you then ground the intuition with the intention, in this case, the same as the one above – "I attract the right people to support me with my purpose and who share my vision".'

Susannah drew a diagram to further explain this concept, showing how *Intuition, Intention* and *Inspired Action* were all interconnected. By listening to his *Intuition*, William could set an *Intention*, which would lead him to act on an *Inspired Action*. Equally by starting with an *Intention*, he would be creating the space for his *Intuition*

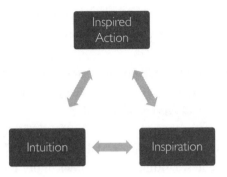

11.2 Intuition – Intention – Inspired Action

to guide him towards *Inspired Action*. After taking the *Inspired Action*, this would then activate further *Intuitions* and *Intentions*.

'And what do you think of the third example I gave you, William? "I lead from the heart with kindness and compassion".' Susannah had added this one in as a stretch for William, but one that would really help him lead more courageously in this new world he was entering into.

'Oh, so it's not just an example then, you want me to really set this as an intention?'

'It's your decision, William,' Susannah clarified. 'You have come a long way in a relatively short period of time and if you really want to bring your purpose and vision alive, then this would be a great intention to hold and if I remember rightly, your description of your "love" value included kindness and compassion.'

'Oh yes, I suppose it does, but it's interesting with my love value, I naturally thought more about this in my personal life.'

'I can understand that, William, and that's natural, but if you want to be completely true to all of your values, then I encourage you to ignite them in all aspects of your life.'

'Well, interestingly enough, on reflection, since I have been igniting my values, I think I have shown more love, kindness and compassion to others and to myself actually. I have been much more conscious of the Self-Care (You to You) side of the Self-Leadership Triangle and the Service (You to Others) side.'

'Leading from the heart encompasses all your values, William, and I would love to see more leaders doing this; it does take real courage. Because when we do, we put our heads above the parapet, we may get judged and some people may ridicule you or put you down, because it shows them where they are not. Yet the rewards that manifest are amazing and by taking this approach, we give other people permission to do the same. Our values are what are most important to us, they are the things we hold most dear, so it makes sense that they reside in our heart. When we get to the true essence of who we all truly are, then leading from the heart is what will bring about transformation on a wider scale.'

'It's time to "let go" of the old ways and bring about the new ways of leading.' Susannah said with an air of excitement, knowing that William was more than ready to lead courageously from the heart.

William was very enthusiastic now and really beginning to experience how powerful this all was. The fact that a deeper meaning, a real purpose to his life and to his leadership were showing up, was giving him a deeper sense of fulfilment.

And it all began with discovering his values. His values were the foundations to all of this. It had to start there. Many people set goals aimlessly without aligning them to their values or vision, which was pointless as far as he could see. It was like building a house and putting the roof on first. His values were his firm foundations, which he was now building everything else from. He committed to Susannah that he would be more conscious about 'leading from his heart with love, kindness and compassion'.

Your Discovery Questions

Now it's your turn to align your goals, intentions and vision.

1. *How are you being tested and which values can you use to support your response?*

2. *What goals are you setting (ensure they are aligned to your values)?*

3. *What intentions could you set to allow your intuition to inspire your actions?*

4. *Do you have a personal and/or professional vision (even if it's still evolving or a just loose idea at present)?*

5. *Which of your values support each of your answers above?*

You may want to record this in your journal.

PART 4

Leading in the New World

'In order to become more of who you truly are, you have to let go of that which you are not.'

12

Energy for Evolution

William had a follow-up meeting with Eric a week after the Senior Leadership Team meeting and was both delighted and surprised that Eric was the one to arrange it. It wasn't completely good news, but at least Eric was showing some interest. Eric had been thinking about what William had said and while he didn't think it was possible within the time frames, he was very impressed with William's new passion, drive and insights. The fact that William was speaking up was just one of the many changes Eric was seeing in William's actions and behaviours. This both pleased him and threatened him a little.

Eric acknowledged William for speaking at the meeting. He respected him for sharing his views and agreed that maybe the culture did leave a lot to be desired and needed to change at a deeper level. He suggested William and Melissa meet to discuss how they could perhaps run a few workshops to announce the new values. This was not William's preferred approach and he felt like Eric was pacifying him a little. Rolling out new values without engaging everyone first was just wallpapering over the cracks. Still, he remembered what Susannah had said and that was to start where the energy for evolution was, and it certainly wasn't with

Eric. So, while he'd not managed to slow the progress of the launch, he would speak to Melissa about changing the roll-out of the training to be more inclusive and wider than originally planned.

It was a step in the right direction, as she'd been open to his idea in the meeting and he knew that Steve would be on board too, so there was definite positive energy amongst some of his peers. He thought for a moment about all the wasted energy there must be in the company – the silos that had been created, the side discussions, people complaining but not taking action, in fact most seemed to be operating on automatic pilot. This gave him hope, as he remembered that it wasn't that long ago that he too was in that space, and look what had happened to him.

What William could be sure of, however, was that there was something he could impact immediately, and that was his own team. There was definitely energy for evolution there. They had noticed the changes he was making in himself and how he was really stepping up as a powerful leader. They had noticed his new found strength and courage and how he had more time for everyone. He was more focused on listening and gaining a deeper understanding of them as individuals and as a team.

Only the other day, Lynne had commented that everyone thought the way William ran team meetings now was so much more uplifting and empowering. Even Russell had mellowed a little; not completely, but their relationship was definitely improving. His team had picked up that he was making changes in his life outside work too; he was happier and much more pleasant to be around. They were keen to know more about what was happening.

LEADING FROM THE INSIDE-OUT

At the beginning of the first team session William made a conscious decision to share his recent journey and be very open and vulnerable with his team. He knew this was the only way to be; to be himself and share from the heart. This could possibly bring about a deeper connection and trust within his team, but that wasn't his driver for doing this. If this was the outcome then fantastic, but the reason he wanted to express his truth was that he was learning the true power of vulnerability.

By sharing from the heart and expressing his truth, he was going to allow his team to see the real William, his true self. He wasn't going to be talking about the actual events of the awards evening because they were all there and saw what happened. No, he would be sharing his inner journey, his realizations, the importance of discovering his values, trusting his intuition and following the energy for evolution. He would speak about the masks he had been wearing, being someone he was not, not really knowing his true self and that he was still learning. And he would also reveal that he had always known that there was another way to be, a way to do things differently and that it had taken something dramatic happening for him to change.

William knew he could be putting himself in a position where he might be judged or ridiculed, but this was a risk he was prepared to take in his new adventure, because, ultimately, being true to himself could only work. If others had issues with it, then it was likely it was their stuff getting in the way, their own masks, projections or expectations and William was letting these go. If he did

205

get impacted, he would just have to deal with it. He now had tools for noticing his triggers, for surrendering the attachments of how others react and letting them go. William trusted, he really trusted more and more, the nudges, the positive messages of reassurance from his intuition telling him to go for it, because he now understood that the rewards would be immense. Not only would he be courageously owning his own personal power, he would be giving others (his team in this instance) permission to do the same. He was beginning to realize just how much of an influence and impact he could have on others by being himself. This gave him more confidence and the courage to continue.

After William had shared his journey with his team, there was an interesting silence. It was not an awkward one at all, but one of respect and admiration. And interestingly for William, as soon as he had consciously ignited his higher priority values more and let go of needing recognition, respect or appreciation, it was showing up much more in his life. It was Lynne who spoke first: 'Thank you for sharing that, William, I am sure it took a lot of courage. It sounds like you have had quite a soul-searching time.'

Ben was still processing all of what William had said. Some of it was lost on him and some was really hitting home, but he decided to speak. 'Well, it's certainly for the best, William,' he added humourously, 'you are much more pleasant to be around now!' Russell remained silent, he was still a little wary of this new approach William was taking. It made him feel uncomfortable, but he had felt listened to by William for the first time in ages the other day, so decided to reserve judgement for now. At the end of the meeting, Sarah said, 'Sounds fantastic. When do we get to do some discovery work on ourselves?'

'I'm glad you asked that, we will start at our next meeting as my coach is going to come and facilitate some sessions for us.'

At their next meeting, they began their first team values discovery session.

Susannah delivered a series of sessions with William's team, helping them to Discover, Define and Ignite their own core values and then to really understand one another's values. They discovered where any potential conflict showed up and how they could collaborate better. Through being values driven, they could see how they would become so much more cohesive as a team and develop deeper levels of trust.

Susannah shared with the team her leading from the inside-out methodology, which she used to engage and align values and develop trust within teams.

This made complete sense to William, based on his own experiences. By understanding his own values he was better placed to relate to others, both personally and professionally. He was pleased he had started with his personal relationships, because making changes at home and being more connected to his family had truly energized him to want to do this with his team. It seemed the team also took this inside-out approach as a more natural way of doing things, and as a result they were more engaged and

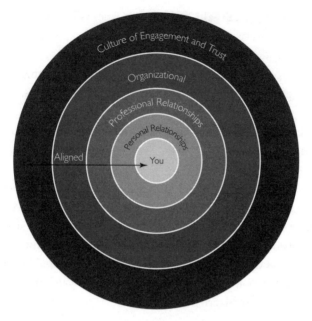

12.1 Leading from the Inside-Out Diagram

productive. They were now bonding deeper as a team, which gave them a much better platform to then look at the company values because each individual would be able to connect with the company values through the lens of their own.

Suddenly everything was falling into place for William. He'd known there was another way and this was it. That's why it also made sense to go where the energy for change and evolution was and work with that.

CREATING A BUZZ

While William had been making all these changes within himself and his team, Beth Calthorpe, Head of Human Resources, was observing him from a distance. Deepti Singh was the HR Business Partner assigned to William's team and she had been engaged in the process from the point when William started bringing about changes within his team. Deepti had fed back to Beth that the transformation that was taking place was remarkable.

People within the team were really coming into their own as they ignited their own values, understood each other more, and defined who worked best in which role and the reasons why. Deepti had observed that the levels of trust were developing to a deep level. And it wasn't just Deepti and Beth that were aware of this. William's peers had started to notice the renewed energy within his team and wondered what he was up to. What was William doing? His team were a lot more upbeat than they had been in ages, the results of his department had increased and William seemed a lot less stressed. In fact, the word 'stress' didn't come into it – there was a real peacefulness and calm about him.

Beth invited William to meet with her for a general review, which happened from time to time, but William didn't expect what was about to come. He hadn't really thought too much about others noticing as he was just so enthused about what he was learning and the impact it was having on him and of those close to him.

Beth greeted him with a smile and said, 'Thanks so much, William, for coming to meet with me.'

'No problem. I know we are due for our review.'

'Well, yes, a review and a little more. I have been very impressed by what I have been observing, both with yourself and your team. It appears you are transforming the culture of the team.

'People are asking me what you are doing and are intrigued. You really have created a buzz!

'I just wanted to congratulate you on starting this change within your team. It certainly is no mean feat, especially when there was no head office initiative.'

Wow! William hadn't even thought about being recognized, something he was once so hung up on when he was operating in the old energies and ways of being. Yet here he was being recognized. He had naturally let go of this desire and Susannah was right – Side 3 of the triangle, Surrender (Others to You) was happening, as if by magic. The more he ignited his values at Side 1, Self-Care (You to You) and Side 2, Service (You to Others), the more life was becoming exciting again.

'You really can't force these things, you have to allow them to flow,' thought William, noticing how different the feeling was when it was unexpected. He also remembered that it was important to 'Receive' when the Surrender (Others to You) Side was given to him. 'Thank you so much,' said William, feeling truly grateful that this had been noticed. He realized how the recognition was now really important, but for different reasons. Being recognized for what he was doing may actually be the way that change would come about.

'May I ask where your renewed enthusiasm came from?' said Beth.

William explained about the awards dinner, which Beth had attended and saw what happened. He knew Beth was also aware of what had happened to Steve, so without breaking the confidentiality of their conversation, he explained how Steve had had a big influence on him, as he saw himself potentially going the same way. He spoke of the work he had done with Susannah and how discovering his core values had changed everything for the best both personally and professionally. He had a totally different view of himself and the world around him and could see possibilities everywhere.

'This is wonderful to hear, William,' said Beth. 'I expect you also met some challenges along the way?'

'For sure! It was a little challenging putting some of the changes into practice because I am now behaving differently. I am having braver conversations and saying "no" to things I would previously have said "yes" to. This has been met with some indifferent reactions, but I just take a deep breath and keep going.

'One of the biggest challenges so far was making the decision to do the values work within my own team, when I didn't have full support or buy-in from other members of the Senior Team, including my boss. It did feel quite scary "going it alone", but the rewards of doing this are proving immense. I would love for this to be company-wide, but when I couldn't get traction for this I decided to do it anyway, because I knew it was the right thing to do.

'I got Susannah to do some work with my team on their individual values and then we looked at our team values. I could have waited and pushed for the company to take a wider approach, yet my team were receptive because they had noticed the changes in me. Something told me to go for it anyway and deal with any consequences later – oh, and the benefits of course.'

'Well there certainly are benefits,' said Beth. 'Kristen Verner has also noticed and would like a conference call with the two of us to discuss how this might work on a larger scale in line with the company rebrand and repositioning.'

William was really taken aback. 'Wow, really?'

'You really are doing a fantastic job, William.'

'Thank you, I really appreciate you telling me. I would be very happy to have a conference call with Kristen, as long as I am not stepping on Eric's toes – I would like to chat with him first.'

'Of course, I understand completely. I agree with you, it is important that we notice where the energy is for change and follow it.'

'I would also like to invite Susannah on to the call, Beth, as she has been an integral part of this transformation.'

'Great! That was going to be my next request. Can you make an introduction for me, William? I would very much like to have a chat with her prior to the conference call. This really is an amazing achievement.'

'Achievement,' thought William, smiling to himself, as he noticed how the intensity of this value had really lessened since discovering the power of his true priority order.

Beth continued. 'And to think I actually thought we were going to lose you at one point. I was convinced you were going to leave and was on the verge of having a chat with you when I started to see some signs of a turnaround. My intuition told me to step back, let you be and observe from a distance.'

'You were right on both counts, Beth,' William said, igniting his honesty value. 'I was speaking to a couple of executive search companies and attended some interviews – one was looking really promising. Then the awards evening happened and the chat with Steve and the coaching with Susannah, and I realized that if I had left as the person I was behaving as back then – the one hiding behind masks, not being true to myself – then I would have been taking that version of me elsewhere and something would have happened at some point. I am sure on reflection that it could have been much worse than what happened at the awards evening.' William realized he must have shifted so much, because now he really did see the awards evening fiasco as a gift and could talk about it openly.

'I was operating in old energies, in ways that didn't serve me, and I have come to realize it is not about changing what's on the outside, it's about looking inside yourself, discovering or rediscovering who we truly are and making changes to be true to that.

I really wished more people realized this stuff and there would be fewer people leaving. Good people would not only be retained, they would excel and organizations would grow and prosper in amazing ways. Also, since discovering their values, some people in my team have shifted roles slightly to suit what they love and allow their values to come more to the fore.'

'This is music to my ears, William,' said Beth in response. 'I have always believed in getting the culture right first, but sometimes I get frustrated with the bureaucracy and the way things have to be done. And it's not just in Gant Foster; I know from colleagues and my previous roles it's common across many organizations.'

NOTICED FROM AFAR

Kristen Verner was the new CEO at Gant Foster and was based in the New York Office. She had been with the company for six months and, unbeknown to William, had been at the awards dinner. She had kept a low profile that evening so as to get a feel for what was happening in the company.

It was important to William to be open and honest with Eric and after sharing what had happened, he went onto his conference call with Kristen.

On the call Kristen told William how she had been present at the awards dinner and had witnessed 'the incident'. William cringed and then laughed. 'Ooh really, I made quite an impact then?!'

Kristen joined in his laughter. 'William, the impact you have made since then is why I wanted this call with you.'

Kristen shared how she had observed and heard great feedback from a number of people about how William had changed personally and what he was now doing with his team. Kristen had joined Gant Foster after the rebrand and repositioning project had begun, but was also having reservations, especially after observing the culture for the past six months. She invited William to offer his views on how things could be different. After William had revealed his own transformation and the work he was doing with his team, he went on to explain his thoughts on the company rebrand and repositioning and how it needed to start inside Gant Foster. 'All employees should know their own values first so they can engage with each other better and then the values of Gant Foster,' he said confidently. 'This is how a new culture will be formed.'

'That makes sense to me,' said Kristen. 'What do you think of Gant Foster's proposed new values?'

William shared with Kristen what he had said in the recent Senior Leadership Team meeting.

Kristen was very intrigued because she had been thinking something similar and hearing him voice this was bringing her own vision to life. She encouraged William to continue.

'We also need to let go of control and this "tell-do" way of operating and develop more care and compassion for one another. To let go of the notion that knowledge is power and allow wisdom and creation through each day. We need to lose the hierarchy structure we currently have and care less about titles and more about heart-centred leadership. For people to be empowered and step into their own authentic leadership power we must find a way to allow them to have a voice, to strip away the masks they are wearing, and let them rediscover who they really are. To be truly values-driven and be in alignment with them in all that we do; our decisions, our communications and our vision, purpose and goals. To listen to our intuition, deep down we do all know what has to be done, but we allow time to pressurize us and it feels too hard to change. We need to create a culture of trust and that starts from the inside-out. Inside each and every one of us first and foremost, inside our teams and inside Gant Foster. Then the energy of what we have created will show on the outside and our clients will reap the benefits tenfold.'

William was shaking, he really didn't know where all that came from. His vision was naturally emerging and it felt good.

'Wow,' said Kristen. 'That was really powerful stuff, William, and extremely good to hear. I love it! What a compelling vision you have there. Wouldn't it be a wonderful world if we could all let go of the things you mentioned and lead authentically with love and compassion for one another. This is certainly how I would like it to be too. We have a way to go, William, but let's hold this vision. You have really given me food for thought here. And, William, never underestimate who you are and what you can achieve by being true to yourself, it's the only way.'

William was delighted with the outcome. Could he really make such an impact on the organization?

After the call William sat quietly taking time to reflect. He realized that the new CEO had noticed and recognized him for his achievements since the awards dinner and yet when he hadn't been striving for achievement or recognition – they had both just been met. Now he really got why they had appeared lower on his values list. He allowed himself to receive these acknowledgements. He had ignited his higher priority values of honesty, security, vitality, love, adventure, feeling free and helping others, and look what had happened! His lower ranked ones of achievement and recognition had also been met and it had been a bit of fun too. He was silently fulfilled. Who knew how this would evolve? He could now see the huge benefits of noticing where the energy was for change, for transformation even, and was following it. He realized that perhaps this traditional top-down approach was a little overrated and another thing that had just been inherited historically as the thing to do. Who was challenging this, he pondered?

Your Discovery Questions

Now it's your turn to notice where you can follow the energy for evolution in your position or company.

1. *What do you need to keep doing regardless of what others do?*

2. *What does your intuition want you to know?*

3. *Where are you regularly living in line with your values?*

4. *Where do you notice the energy for evolution in yourself? Your team? Your organization?*

5. *Where does your energy feel light/heavy? (This gives a clue to what the right choice is for you.)*

13

Staying on the Path

Illiam didn't really need further confirmation that staying at Gant Foster was the right choice, but it was lovely that the conversation with Kristen had solidified this. What if he had left? He didn't even want to go there. He had made the right decision, which he knew intuitively, and then consciously checking in with his values had confirmed it.

He discussed this with Susannah during one of his monthly momentum sessions: 'I can't imagine what I would have been like if I had left, I would never have discovered all of this.'

'You may have,' said Susannah, 'at another time or in another way.'

William laughed. 'Oh yes and a few more "smacks in the face", I would have gone through the same cycle over again until something bigger ...,' he stopped himself. 'Well, I am not going to go there.'

'You chose the path that was right for you at this point in time, William. For others, the right decision may have been to leave; but it is doing this work, as you are experiencing now, that put you in a much more empowered place to make an informed and conscious choice that you know is right for you.'

Now, he knew this didn't mean everything would be smooth sailing. There would be more tests, challenges and learnings on the path he had chosen. He knew these would lead to more realizations and growth opportunities and he was embracing it all. There were also rewards, the sense of fulfilment and the magic that living and leading in line with your values brings, together with trusting your intuition and following the energy for evolution.

HEALTHY BOUNDARIES

William was learning what to consciously say 'yes' to and 'no' to. He was creating healthy boundaries in his life. For example, his family time was sacred and he intended it to stay that way. He was learning more and more to trust his intuition and go with it, even when it made no logical sense. In fact, especially when it made no logical sense. His intuition was his guide, his servant and his manifestor. His values enabled him to consciously stay on course and help him in times of challenge, and joy for that matter. William was no longer restless from frustration and stress, he now had a purpose, a vision to bring about transformation – this was a new kind of restlessness and one that drove him in a very positive way.

A restless feeling ...

William was now restless for a very different reason. He felt alive, excited and energized, and this new restless feeling was now his driver. He felt he had found his calling. It wasn't outside of him, he didn't need to go anywhere else, it was inside of him and now he had ignited the flame he felt like he was on fire. He was a different person; he was being his true self, most of the time. The awards evening felt like a distant memory even though it was only a few months ago. William would never have thought this much change, transformation even, was possible in such a relatively short space of time. He knew the journey didn't stop here and he would need to rely on his core values and trust his intuition to allow him to flow through future challenges.

William was excited about challenging the status quo, questioning the norm, the mundane and perceptions of what was expected. He was well aware after his own soul awakening moment that most people around him were walking around half asleep, unhappy and most definitely unfulfilled. He could see why Susannah was so passionate about the work she did and now it was his turn to take the baton into Gant Foster. And while he wasn't about to become a professional coach, he was ready to combine what he had learned through his own coaching with his business experience and step into New World Leadership; he would take on the role of a pioneer and find his way, allowing it to evolve as he went.

There was a time when he would have needed greater clarity about what was in store before he took action, but the more he practised 'being present in the moment' and stepping into his recently discovered adventure value, the more he was trusting himself to be open and allowing things to evolve.

His original restless feeling was one that something was missing, yet there was nothing missing at all. What was needed was a rediscovery of who he was and what was most important to him. This new feeling of restlessness was one of excitement; he now had more meaning and purpose in his life and wanted to influence change in those around him.

From routine to rituals

When William woke in the morning he no longer had to 'snooze' his alarm clock because he was awake and out of bed before it went off. He didn't check his smart phone either. He would start his day with some quiet time thinking of three things he was grateful for in that moment. He would meditate for 20 minutes, though he was still getting used to this because occasionally thoughts would drift in and he sometimes got distracted. But he was learning to let them come and go.

William was really enjoying his self-development time. He would read and journal before taking a shower and having a healthy breakfast. He was also building exercise into his daily routines – either a walk, cycle ride or swim. He noticed that when he started his day in this way he was calmer and could deal with things with ease.

On the occasions when he let outside pressures affect him and he didn't carry out his morning ritual, he noticed a big difference in how his day went. He would be more on edge and less patient with things. This contrast made him even more committed to honouring his sacred morning time. It no longer felt like a routine; this was something he was doing with conscious intention. He now got why it was so important to honour Self-Care (You to You) at Side 1 of the Self-Leadership Triangle, first.

Letting go of the old – bringing in the new

William was progressing well, yet realized he still had much to learn. There was no point waiting to perfect everything, he was a work in progress after all, and while sometimes it wasn't comfortable, he found putting his new skills and tools into action was the best way of learning, developing and course correcting.

William continued to gain great benefit from his monthly coaching sessions with Susannah, sharing his developments and then being supported and challenged by her to take the next step. He found his confidence was increasing each time they met and was actually learning to let go of what others thought of him or expected of him. He felt he was no longer operating at the 'Others to You' side of the Triangle of Self-Leadership, or at least he was noticing it more and could course-correct.

If he felt triggered by something or usually someone, he would check in and see which value was impacted. Sometimes just the awareness was enough for him to surrender the feeling and let it go. Sometimes he would need to go a bit deeper to see if he was running a rule that didn't serve him.

During his next coaching session, Susannah had suggested that they focus on what else he needed to 'let go of' in order to move forwards into this new way of leading. What would no longer serve him? What might hold him back from living and leading in line with his values and purpose?

Susannah and William worked through his thoughts and he decided that he needed to let go of the following:

- Old patterns that no longer served him; he was góing to consciously replace reaction with intention. He had already changed his morning routine to a morning ritual.

- Beating himself up was to be replaced by being kinder and more forgiving to himself.

- What others think, or at least his perceptions of what others were thinking, and trust his intuition and act accordingly.

- Replacing habits and beliefs. He had chosen to replace one of his morning coffees with a herbal tea. He might cut caffeine out altogether, but for now reducing his intake was good progress. He was letting go of his habitual 'I have to work hard' belief and allowing himself to be more in the present and put the important things first. And he was making more time for his family.

- Identifying himself by his achievements, material possessions and his title. Did it matter what he had accumulated and that he was Operations Director? That wasn't where the real power lay. No, that lay inside.

- Old ways of operating and structures that no longer served him; he would challenge the status quo more and express his truth to bring about change.

- Ego-based decisions, thoughts and actions and lead from his heart and soul, because that was where his true self resided.

- Low-level emotions – turning fear into courage, guilt into forgiveness and anger and frustration into love.

- Being attached to the outcome of how things happen and let them unfold naturally – to notice the energy. No more controlling things to go a certain way.

These would all be works in progress and he would need to course-correct as he went. Susannah encouraged him to continue to journal new insights and awareness's, to 'let go' of anything that no longer served him and replace with the new methodologies and ways of being he had learned, so he could lead more and more courageously in this 'new world' of leadership.

What does success mean to you?

William now had a very different meaning of what success meant to him, one that was much more authentic. He thought back to when he first started the coaching with Susannah, which was only a couple of months ago, and was amazed at how much he had changed – yes, he had actually transformed: he was a different person to the one he was being, well pretending to be, before igniting his values. Was it any wonder he had struggled to define success? He didn't know who he was then and now he was really beginning to. His definition of success now was 'To be fulfilled in every possible moment, know who I am, be true to myself and lead courageously, to stay on this new, exciting and adventurous path that I have chosen.'

Your Discovery Questions

Now it's your turn to Lead in the New World. Enjoy answering this final set of questions. The answers will help you to be your true self even more.

1. *What do you need to put in place to remain true to yourself?*

2. *What rituals are you adopting in your life?*

3. *What will you decide to let go of?*

4. *What do you want to say 'Yes' and 'No' to?*

5. *What does success now mean to you?*

6. *Where can you positively challenge the status quo?*

7. *What will you do when your restlessness shows up?*

From Restless
Executive to
Courageous Leader

This is a summary of the process that William went through on his journey of transformation from Restless Executive to Courageous Leader ...

1. Identifying his restlessness.

2. Owning his 'moment of realization'.

3. Committing to taking action and making changes.

4. Discovering his core values and learning how to fully honour them.

5. Trusting his intuition.

6. Following the energy for evolution.

7. Stepping into his courage and taking a leap of faith.

Epilogue

William knew it was time to step up and lead the change Gant Foster needed. He had practised his new skills and felt empowered and ready to take a leap of faith. He discovered that for him, a meaningful career was less about the trappings of being an Operations Director and more about being an authentic leader and being true to himself and his values. The job title didn't matter anymore – his soul was calling and he felt compelled to act. Of course, William didn't have all the answers, but he was certain things had to change and in his mind he questioned why people in the company weren't operating differently. Why did they act like robots, doing exactly what they were told? Why did they simply accept all the initiatives from head office and continue to do what was expected of them without considering the consequences?

William was now tuned to sense when people were running on automatic mode, remaining stuck in their ways and not being true to themselves. Occasionally the status quo would be challenged, but from what place? For the greater good of Gant Foster or simply to satisfy a personal need? Heck, some people would make a challenge just for the hell of it – what was the point of that? William wondered. If they could just be shown how to be more purposeful. If his fellow leaders truly knew themselves better and understood their core values, they could collaborate to ensure the company moved forward more positively. Everyone would benefit.

William knew he had to lead the shift for the company to become truly values driven from the inside-out. This was both a scary and an exciting thought, but William was learning to trust and follow his intuition. He must do this for the right reasons rather than just to satisfy his ego. And it certainly wouldn't be easy because people are brought up to try and fit in rather than to be themselves. What would others think of him for leading this movement? Those old feelings of not being good enough kept surfacing, but William knew he had the courage to address them and he had a new 'moment of realization' – that he was now *restless* to get going with it.

A new paradigm of leadership was emerging and William had seen a glimpse of what life could be like both personally and professionally. He sometimes found all the excitement he was feeling a little overwhelming – and to think, just a few months ago he had been prepared to leave the company! He was so glad he had chosen this route, to stay put and lead the change himself. But, where would he start? What came first? He really needed to think this through and allow things to emerge naturally. William smiled to himself – 'allow things to emerge' – he certainly was changing. He could feel the push–pull between wanting to do things quickly and knowing that for change to be sustainable, the pace must be slower. People would have to engage in the process and he'd need to be patient. It would be a long journey to take Gant Foster on and it wouldn't happen overnight, but he would make a start with his own team. Everything has to begin with a first step, he mused.

AN INVITATION FOR YOU – THE LEADER

- This is your time to step into that place of courage, to lead from your heart and own your true leadership power
- Let go of ego-based thoughts and actions to Discover, Define and Ignite your values
- Be guided by and honour your intuition
- Notice, then follow where the energy is for evolution

WILL YOU GO THERE?

WILL YOU ANSWER THE CALL OF YOUR RESTLESSNESS?

WILL YOU?

There is no time like the present. I call you forth on your own leadership adventure and I wish you joy, awareness and deep fulfilment.

In love and service to you, The Leader.

Jo x

More Resources

... to help you transform from a Restless Executive to a Courageous Leader in the New World

Now that you have finished reading William Cleverley's story and journey of transformation, it's your turn to embody these changes as part of your daily life.

To support you with this and to access the resources mentioned in this book (Priority Order, Rules Worksheets, Conflict Loop, Self Leadership Triangle) including video content and more, please go to:

www.TheRestlessExecutive.com/resources

To find out more about Jo, her retreats or to book her for speaking events, please visit her at:

www.josimpson.com

Stay connected and follow Jo and her latest updates at:

Twitter: @josimpsonspeaks
Facebook: The Restless Executive
Linked In: uk.linkedin.com/in/josimpson

Making a Positive Difference in the World

If you have been inspired by 'The Restless Executive' and want to support others on their journey and help Jo to honour her own values and mission, here are some ways you can do that –

- Gift *The Restless Executive* to your friends, family and colleagues at work

- Share your thoughts about *The Restless Executive* on Twitter, Facebook, in Blogs or write a book review

- Create a study group to work through *The Restless Executive* together, helping each other and sharing experiences

- If you are responsible for developing people within your organization, you can invest in copies of this book for all your Leaders, Managers and Teams

About the Author

J o Simpson has a unique talent for transforming 'Restless Executives' into courageous modern leaders.

Her career of over 25 years holds an impressive track record, much of it spent leading training teams and delivering education programmes in the banking sector across Europe, the USA and Asia Pacific.

In the early 2000s, Jo challenged her own "Restlessness", sparking a fast track period of personal and professional transformation.

After qualifying as a professional coach, Jo moved to Dubai in 2005, where she established Coaching and Mentoring Middle East LLC. This groundbreaking company was instrumental in transforming the management culture of numerous local and international organizations.

Jo is an engaging keynote speaker and executive leadership coach and since returning to the UK in 2010, she continues to pioneer her methodologies for values-based leadership and innovative team development.

The Restless Executive shares Jo's first-hand experience that the key to lasting empowerment and transformation for leaders and their teams lies in aligning with their core values to become the intuitive, enlightened leaders of today's new business paradigm.

When not busy transforming the corporate world, Jo loves dancing, learning to play the clarinet and spending time in nature, especially walking in the countryside, being by the ocean and skiing in the mountains.

To keep in touch with Jo and learn more about how to transform your restlessness, register to receive her regular blogs and 'Lead as You' tips at www.josimpson.com

Acknowledgements

My deepest gratitude goes to my Mum and Dad, for your unwavering support, belief and unconditional love especially when I chose 'an alternative path'.

To Simon for your unconditional love, for supporting me in so many ways and for believing in me, especially when I didn't.

There are more people to thank than I have space to individually mention here, family and friends for their encouragement and support, the fantastic team at Wiley, my Coaches, Mentors, Mastermind groups and Fellow Speakers.

A huge Thank You to all my clients that I have had the privilege to serve over the years. It is an honour to be able to support you on your journeys. Without you, I wouldn't be able to show up in the world and do what I do.

A few special mentions are due to Christiane, Dave, Helena, Lisa, Molly, Nick, Rachael, Sylvia, Tamar and Will – your help, dedication, love and support both to me and in birthing this book into the world has been immensely humbling, fun and has truly demonstrated the power of a values-driven team.